☾ HALLOWEEN ☽

HALLOWEEN

From Pagan Ritual to Party Night

Nicholas Rogers

OXFORD
UNIVERSITY PRESS

2 0 0 2

OXFORD

UNIVERSITY PRESS

Oxford   New York
Auckland   Bangkok   Buenos Aires   Cape Town   Chennai
Dar es Salaam   Delhi   Hong Kong   Istanbul   Karachi   Kolkata
Kuala Lumpur   Madrid   Melbourne   Mexico City   Mumbai   Nairobi
São Paulo   Shanghai   Singapore   Taipei   Tokyo   Toronto

and an associated company in
Berlin

Copyright © 2002 by Oxford University Press, Inc.

Published by Oxford University Press, Inc.
198 Madison Avenue, New York, New York 10016

www.oup.com

Oxford is a registered trademark of Oxford University Press

Library of Congress Cataloging-in-Publication Data
Rogers, Nicholas, 1944–
Halloween : from pagan ritual to party night / Nicholas Rogers.
p. cm.
Includes bibliographical references and index.
ISBN 0–19–514691–3
1. Halloween—History. I. Title

GT4965 .R634 2002
394.2646—dc21   2002017061

3 5 7 9 8 6 4 2

Printed in the United States of America
on acid-free paper

For Daniel, Kate, and Vanessa

CONTENTS

ACKNOWLEDGMENTS

The idea for this book grew out of a York University conference that I organized in April 1995 with my colleague, Adrian Shubert, on the subject of Spectacle, Monument, and Memory. I would like to thank all the people who commented on my paper at that meeting and subsequently at the Celtic Studies conference at St. Michael's College, Toronto, in October 1995, and at the School for American Research in Santa Fe, New Mexico, in March 1996. Their suggestions helped me develop the arguments in the book and expand its horizons.

I would also like to thank the Head of the Department of Irish Folklore, University College, Dublin, for permission to quote extracts from the archives of the Irish Folklore Commission of 1941–42; and Patricia Fulton, the archivist of the Folklore and Language Archive at the Memorial University of Newfoundland, for permission to use materials pertaining to Halloween in its collection. May I also thank the *Detroit Free Press* for permission to reprint a cartoon by Bill Day on the subject of Devil's Night, and my daughter, Katherine Greenslade Rogers, for providing me with several photos of trick-or-treating in Montreal. Every effort was made to contact the owners of the copyright on the *Halloween* film stills, Galaxy International Releasing Company, but no reply was forthcoming.

In writing a book of this nature I have inevitably incurred many debts. I am grateful to the New York Public Library, the Chicago Public Library, the University of Michigan Library at Ann Arbor, the Huntington Library at San Marino, California, the Stauffer Library at Queen's University, Kingston, Ontario, and, nearer home, to the interlibrary loan of the Scott Library at York University, the Jason Robarts Library at the University of Toronto, especially the microtext section, and to the Film Reference Library in Toronto. They gave me access to a host of books, pamphlets, prints, and newspapers that were necessary to the writing of this book.

In addition to these libraries, many individuals provided me with new sources of information and sometimes offered personal reminiscences of their youthful Halloweens. Among those who helped in this way are Bill Beezley, Joseph Boyle, Betsy Broun, Patrick Connor, Ramsay Cook, Bill Dyck, Jonathan Edmondson, Sabina Flanagan, Susan Foote, Scott Forsyth, Yves Frenette, Gerry Hallowell, Jeet Heer, Victoria Heftler, Craig Heron, Philip Hiscock, Gregory and Linda Kealey, Saul Kendal, Marilyn Morris, Denis Paz, Adele Perry, Chandra Persaud, Bryan Palmer, Wilf Prest, Ian Radforth, Roy Ritchie, Catherine Saxburg, John Short, Marc Stein, David Thompson, Keith Walden, Helen Wilcox, and Cynthia Wright. I thank them all for their help, as I do Matt Cohen and Mark Flumerfelt, who both made some initial searches of newspaper sources for me.

This book was initially written in the summer of 1999 in Toronto and at Sangster Lake, just north of Kingston. It was then read by Bryan Palmer, Nicole Tellier, and David A. Wilson. I am very grateful to them for taking the time to do this and for their criticisms and encouragement. Although I did not always heed their comments, they prompted me to think of ways of refining the argument and of expanding the scope of the book to include a chapter on the Day of the Dead.

In getting this book to press I also incurred other debts. John Dawson of the Instructional Technology Centre at York managed to clean up my prints, some of which were taken from old microfilm. And the staff of Oxford University Press, especially Susan Ferber and Joellyn Ausanka, helped me translate my typescript into what I hope will be a readerly book. I thank them for their guidance, encouragement, and help.

Finally, I would like to dedicate this book to my children. Although I do not think that Halloween has ever been simply a children's night, the fun of watching them dress up and trick-or-treat still resonates in my memory.

☾ HALLOWEEN ☉

introduction

In 1998, my partner and I decided to leave the tricksters at our door and venture downtown to the gay quarter of Toronto. For many years now, the gay parades to the St. Charles tavern, one of the highlights of Halloween in the 1970s, had disappeared; they had been displaced by the emergence of Gay Pride Day as a celebration of homosexual affirmation. In the last few years, the main Halloween action could be found on Yonge Street, where youthful revelers rocked cars that were locked in the traffic and paraded along the sidewalk to the honking of horns and the flashing of cameras. Witches, demons, devils, clowns, Draculas, and Frankenstein's monsters all walked the walk, and, very occasionally, at the intersection of Church and Wellesley, in particular, one could catch a glimpse of Beauty and the Beast, or a meticulously dressed Marie Antoinette, on their way to a private party. But in 1998, the revelers were out in force for Masquer Aid. Two blocks of Church Street had been cordoned off, and the costumes glistened in the neon lights.

At Slack Alice's Bar and Grill, we encountered our first Monica Lewinsky of the night. She had all the gear: the beret, the blue semen-stained dress, the presidential cigar. In our corner of the bar cross-dressers abounded: women dressed as pirates, bejewelled ladies with party masks, a six-foot-one Joan Crawford sporting a cigarette

Monica Lewinsky
look-alike, Toronto
Masquer Aid, 1998.
Photo by Nick Rogers.

holder and a fox fur, and a half man–half woman who reminded me
of a mock-portrait of the Chevalier d'Eon, a French diplomat whose
sexuality was the source of much speculation in the London of the
1770s.[1] Amid the throbbing strobe lights there was a three-headed
Mount Rushmore and two cowboys whose silver-painted torsos self-
evidently spoke of gymwork. As the tempo of the evening rose, they
would clamber on the bar and strut their stuff to good-humored
applause.

By 10 P.M. the street carnival was in full swing. There were men on
stilts and dominos out of Fellini's *Casanova*. There were mounties,
spider women, Darth Vaders, a Zorro, and a King of Hearts. At Wilde

Half man–half woman,
Toronto Masquer Aid,
1998. *Photo by Nick
Rogers.*

Oscar's bar we encountered an Edward Scissorhands. Nuns and angels
graced the evening's promenade, just as they would in Greenwich
Village. They rubbed shoulders with samurai and road warriors, one of
whom wore biker leggings that bared his ass. A transvestite in a fur coat
periodically flashed virtually everything, her silicone-stocked breasts
and genitals covered only by pom-poms. Not to be upstaged, a cluster
of drag queens wheeled in a giant penis ringed with tinsel. More
demurely, a handful of swells in evening dress performed the sinking
of the *Titanic*, clutching large styrofoam chips of ice as they collectively
sank to the pavement. As we left the masquerade around midnight, I
saw them pulsating to the beat on a dance floor off Gloucester Mews.

Edward Scissorhands,
Toronto Masquer Aid,
1998. *Photo by Nick
Rogers.*

Halloween at the end of the millennium has become a major party
night for adults, arguably the most important after New Year's Eve.
An estimated 65 percent of American adults participate in Halloween,
beyond, that is, simply handing out candy. Roughly $1.5 billion is spent
every year on costumes, and a further $3 billion on party accessories.[2]
In fact, the amount of money spent on Halloween has more than
doubled in the last decade, making it the second retail bonanza after
Christmas. The holiday has become a sort of continental Mardi Gras,
usually more free-form and spontaneous than the elaborately staged
Mardi Gras festivals of New Orleans and Mobile, whose street parades
are carefully regulated by local societies and where the boundaries

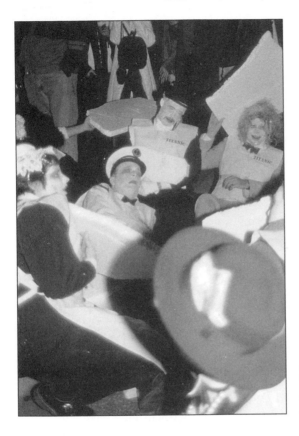

Going down with the
Titanic, Toronto
Masquer Aid, 1998.
Photo by Nick Rogers.

between performers and spectators are more clearly drawn. What is it about Halloween that disposes people to dress up and act out their individual fantasies, some purely fanciful, others more self-consciously political? What does it tell us about the body politics of the late twentieth century? Is Halloween quintessentially a children's celebration that has been appropriated by adults? Or is the history of this ancient festival rather more complex? And how can we explain not only its ongoing popularity but also its emergence in the twentieth century as a North American festival that successfully transcended its ethnic roots? It is these kinds of questions that this cultural history attempts to address.

My own fascination with Halloween stems from a long-standing scholarly interest in crowds and urban festivals. It is also based on the fact that as a child I never experienced Halloween. Although I can lay claim to some Celtic heritage, the part of Britain from which I hail never observed the 31st of October. In the southern reaches of Somerset, at a little village called Hinton St. George, there was and still is a festival called Punky or Spunky Night, so named after the turnip jack-o'-lanterns that were carved into grotesque faces to represent imps or goblins. On the last Thursday in October, children visit local houses with their lighted lanterns, performing a festive repertoire that is very similar to a North American Halloween.[3] Yet in most West Country towns and villages, Halloween was unknown, at least until quite recently. The real night of autumnal festivities occurred a few days later, on Bonfire Night, historically the English anniversary of the so-called Gunpowder Plot. This was the night of bonfires and fireworks, of youthful revelry and innumerable pranks, although sometimes the mischief occurred on the evening before. Coming to Canada in my early twenties, I was bewildered by Halloween, a North American festival about which I knew nothing. And as I learned the rituals along with my children and witnessed the efflorescence of the festival in the 1970s and 1980s—and the controversies it provoked—my wonderment increased. This book is in part an attempt to make sense of that story and to assess the holiday's wider cultural significance.

It begins with some discussion of origins, the automatic reflex of the historian, although one that is sometimes suspected of privileging a developmental perspective that overlooks the ruptures and strangeness of the past. In fact, I do not invest a great deal of interpretive significance in the quest for Halloween's origins, save only to illustrate and understand how people have appropriated parts of Halloween's past in fashioning their own meaning of the holiday. Chapter 1 looks at Halloween's purported pagan origins, a theme of particular interest to new-age enthusiasts, to Hollywood, and to those of the evangelical Right who denounce the holiday as satanic. Chapter 2 explores more closely Halloween's religious origins and practices, its cultural links with other early modern festivals, and its tortuous and uneven survival in post-reformation Britain. The scene then shifts in chapter 3 to the other side of the Atlantic, where I show how nineteenth-century immigrants from Ireland and Scotland remodeled the holiday and how it broke free from its Celtic moorings to acquire a permanent place in the North American calendar of anniversaries. Here I argue that Halloween's capacity to provide a public space for social inversion or transgression held it in good stead at a time when other potentially raucous holidays were becoming more institutionalized and domesticated. In particular, Halloween gave a broad range of people the opportunity to reclaim the city streets from its corporate owners and boosters, however temporarily, and to represent the marginal, the unorthodox, and, above all, the wild energy of youth.[4]

The remaining chapters of the book explore this theme more fully in the context of the mid- to late-twentieth century, when Halloween became a more commercialized event within mass culture. Chapter 4 explores the attempts to reorder the holiday as a children's festival and the degree to which this was undermined by urban disquiet and decay, in particular, by the circulation of urban legends about Halloween sadists. Chapter 5 looks at the way in which Hollywood has sought to capture Halloween and the extent to which the holiday has become a fright night of simulated horror, in which the distinction between the real and "phoney real" has become radically scrambled.

The next chapter of the book examines the revival of Halloween as an adult festival at the end of the twentieth century. Here I assess the potential of Halloween as a space for social transgression and parody at a time when leisure has become so routinized and commercial. In particular, I stress the emergence of Halloween as a new site for gender politics, not simply because the holiday affords an opportunity to flout gender norms in traditional society, but because it has been used to reaffirm the values of feminist and gay cultures. Yet if modern-day Halloween increasingly celebrates difference, it also represents

American-ness. This is especially true for immigrants to North America, but it is also the case in countries where American culture is aggressively marketed. In the penultimate chapter I look at Halloween in the context of the Southwest and Mexico, where Halloween is juxtaposed to a cognate festival, the Day of the Dead. Will the growing presence of Halloween south of the Rio Grande undermine the vitality and meaning of *El Dia de los Muertos*, to the detriment of Mexican cultural traditions? Or is it possible to imagine a fruitful exchange between these two festivals, perhaps even a new hybrid? This cultural engagement, particularly the issue of why *El Dia de los Muertos* commemorates the dead in a way that Halloween does not, helps frame the last chapter, where I discuss the celebration of Halloween in the United States in the wake of the terrorist attacks on September 11.

To examine the history of Halloween is to recognize that it is not a holiday that has been celebrated the same way over the centuries, nor one whose meaning is fixed. If it is a fixture in our annual calendar, it is also a holiday that has been reinvented in different guises over the centuries. Those reinventions can be related to the changing demographic regimes of the past; to the making of different ethnic, national, and sexual identities; to the shifting social and political anxieties of late twentieth-century America; and to the commercialization of leisure with which Halloween is now very much associated. As a holiday without an official patron, Halloween has never been securely anchored in national narratives. It has always operated on the margins of mainstream commemorative practices, retaining some of the topsy-turvy features of early modern festivals—parody, transgression, catharsis, the bodily excesses of the carnivalesque—and recharging them in new social and political contexts. That is part of the secret of its resilience and vibrancy.

☾ 1 ☾

SAMHAIN

and the Celtic Origins of Halloween

Halloween is commonly thought to have pagan origins, even though its etymology is Christian. Halloween is, quite literally, the popular derivative of All Hallow Even, or the eve of All Saints' Day (1 November). Taken together with All Souls' Day, which falls on 2 November, it is a time assigned in the Christian calendar for honoring the saints and the newly departed. In past centuries, it was also the occasion for praying for souls in purgatory. Yet because Halloween is popularly associated with the supernatural, it is often believed to have strong pagan roots that were never eliminated by the holiday's subsequent Christianization.

Some folklorists have detected its origins in the Roman feast of Pomona, the goddess of fruits and seeds, or in the festival of the dead called Parentalia. More typically, it has been linked to the Celtic festival of Samhain or Samuin (pronounced sow-an or sow-in), meaning summer's end. In the tenth-century Gaelic text *Tochmarc Emire*, the heroine Emer mentions Samhain as the first of the four quarter days in the medieval Irish calendar, "when the summer goes to its rest."[1] Paired with the feast of Beltane, which celebrated the life-generating powers of the sun, Samhain beckoned to winter and the dark nights ahead. It was quintessentially "an old pastoral and agricultural festival," wrote

J. A. MacCulloch, "which in time came to be looked upon as affording assistance to the powers of growth in their conflict with the powers of blight."[2] The feast of Samhain was the occasion of stock-taking and in-gathering, of reorganizing communities for the winter months, including the preparation of quarters for itinerant warriors and shamans. It was also a period of supernatural intensity, when the forces of darkness and decay were said to be abroad, spilling out from the *sidh,* the ancient mounds or barrows of the countryside. To ward off these spirits, the Irish built huge, symbolically regenerative bonfires and invoked the help of the gods through animal and perhaps even human sacrifice.

Not all writers agree on precisely what went on at the feast of Samhain, but many stress its elemental primitivism and its enduring legacy to the character of Halloween, particularly in terms of its omens, propitiations, and links to the otherworld. Although the divinatory practices associated with Halloween have long since disappeared, the holiday's netherworld resonances are still reproduced in jack-o'-lanterns and ghoulish garb. Indeed, in recent years the supernatural qualities of Halloween have been revitalized by two opposing groups: new-age pagans and the religious Right. The first has stressed the "natural uncanniness" of Halloween and its therapeutic qualities in helping people "touch the realms of myth and imagination" and "come to terms with their fears of change and death."[3] The Christian evangelists, in contrast, have denounced its "satanism" and its glorification of evil. Some have even claimed that Halloween is "one of the four black sabbaths when witches meet to worship the devil."[4] Not surprisingly, they have urged school boards to ban Halloween celebrations because of the day's flagrantly un-Christian overtones.

In the meantime, entrepreneurs, eager to cash in on the scariest night of the year, are not averse to replicating the nastiest narratives of Samhain. In the wave of Halloween horror movies over the past two decades, this ancient Celtic festival has been invoked. Although John Carpenter's cult horror movie *Halloween* made no reference to ancient Celtic rites, the same was not true of its sequels. In *Halloween 2,* during the hunt for the psychotic serial killer Michael Myers, someone smears SAMHAIN on a school wall. It is a sign that prompts Myers's former analyst, Dr. Sam Loomis, to expound on the Druidic sacrifices of animals and humans in an attempt to foretell the future through their "contorted bodies." In *Halloween 3*, a crazed manufacturer of Irish descent (Conal Cochran) contrives to immolate children by inserting a life-threatening force from Stonehenge into their Halloween masks. By the sixth, *Halloween: The Curse of Michael Myers*, even the medical establishment of Myers's former hospital has been infected with the Samhain bug, quite ready to appease the life force through a black mass and the ritual sacrifice of an infant child. Here the film toys with the notion that Samhain involved a macabre rite in which first-born children were sacrificed to the gods of darkness. Whatever new-age devotees might think about Samhain's gentler, therapeutic qualities, its savagery has been marketable.

We can dismiss the argument that Samhain was "satanic" or that in some essentialist sense Halloween is a "satanic ritual," as the Reverend Pat Robertson, the founder of the Christian Coalition, declared in 1982.[5] Although a few pre-Christian religions depicted a dualistic struggle between the God of Light and the God of Darkness, Satanism is essentially a Christian creation, a travesty of Christian forms centered on the fallen rebel angel, Lucifer. In fact, the monism of the early Christian church left little room for Satan. His infernal majesty made his entrance in the Book of Job, appeared more frequently in the New Testament, and came to the fore only in the writings of St. Augustine. Certainly, Satanism was incompatible with the polytheism of the ancient Celts. Indeed, the belief in satanic cults blossomed only in the late medieval era when it formed part of the persecutory discourse against heretics and witches—long after the demise of Samhain.[6]

The issue of whether or not the celebrants of Samhain appeased the gods with animal or human sacrifice is, however, more contentious. Although some of the Celtic folklore hints at sacrificial rites involving humans, the main literary evidence is derived from the classical authors of the first century before Christ. These writers, including Julius Caesar, Strabo, and Diodorus, decried the practice of human sacrifice at a time when the Roman world no longer thought it compatible with civilization. These were not first-hand accounts but scholarly ruminations on the beliefs, superstitions, and practices of the "barbarous peoples" north of the Alps. Moreover, they were mainly negative constructs prompted by what the authors saw as dramatic affronts to civilized society. As such, they might tell us more about the Romans than about their warring neighbors of northern Europe.[7]

None of these accounts specifically mentions Samhain, either. Their focus was altogether more general, referring only to the execrable practices of the Gauls, or the Keltoi, and to the seers or Druids who officiated over them. It is by way of the Druids that the link to Samhain has been made, on the assumption that they were the principal officiators of sacrificial rites in the Celtic north and that their rites were intrinsic to Samhain, as they were to other quarterly festivals.

The idea that the Druids engaged in human sacrifice is not implausible, although the references to their activities are frustratingly fleeting. The most detailed account of a Druidic ceremony comes from Pliny the Elder (23 or 24–70 A.D.), but it concerns the sacrifice of two white bulls on the sixth day of the moon in what was very likely a routine fertility rite rather than a special ceremony.[8] Pliny thought the affair pretty trivial, and condescendingly remarked that "such are the religious feelings that are entertained towards trifling things by many peoples." Unfortunately, neither he nor his near contemporaries were prepared to elaborate upon the public rites of more festive occasions. Writers from previous generations, such as Strabo of Amasia and Diodorus of Sicily, were more forthcoming. Diodorus was especially intrigued by the Druidic practice of stabbing victims and auguring from their death-throes. "When the stricken victim has fallen," he remarked, "they read the future from the manner of his fall and from the twitching of his limbs, as well as from the gushing of the blood, having learned to place confidence in an ancient and long-continued practice of observing such matters."[9] Strabo made the same observations about divining from the "death struggle," although he also referred to death by impalement or arrow, even though archery was not a normal part of Celtic warfare. The Roman historian Tacitus was more graphic in his *Annals*. He denounced the "savage cults" of the Druids, specifically their propensity to "slake the altars with captive blood and to consult their deities by means of human entrails."[10]

Without a doubt, the most dramatic account of human sacrifice came from the pens of Strabo, Julius Caesar, and Diodorus, all of whom referred to the huge human-like wicker structures into which living men were cast before they perished in fire. The Druids, claimed Caesar, believed "that unless for a man's life a man's life be paid, the majesty of the immortal gods may not be appeased; and in public, as in private life, they observe an ordinance of sacrifices of the same kind. Others use figures of immense size, whose limbs, woven out of twigs, they fill with living men and set on fire, and the men perish in a sheet of flame."[11] This extraordinary account, very likely derived from the Syrian historian Posidonius, so captivated the Englishman Aylett Sammes that in his *Britannia Antiqua Illustrata* of 1676, he commissioned an engraving of the wicker man for his readers, "the strangeness of which Custome I have here thought not amiss to represent."[12] Predictably, it is an image that has made a comeback in Halloween horror drama, forming the sinister subtext to the British-made production *The Wicker Man* (1973), which has become something of a cult movie in the United States.

Admirers of the Druids have sought to dispel the accuracy of these accounts by emphasizing their second, even third-hand derivation, and their very obvious propagandist value to the Roman imperial war effort. It was predictable that the Romans should charge the Keltoi with barbaric habits that they themselves had publicly repudiated in an attempt to vindicate their own conquests and improve troop morale. Strabo even attributed cannibalism and incest to the barbarous Celts. "They count it an honourable thing, when their fathers die, to devour them, and openly have intercourse, not only with other women, but

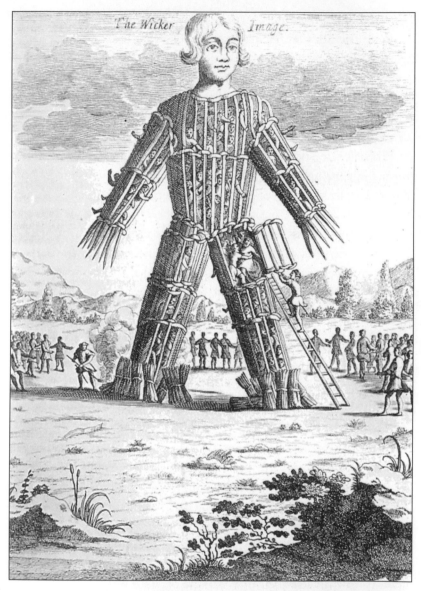

The Wicker Man, from Aylett Sammes, *Britannia Antiqua Illustrata* (1676).

also with their mothers and sisters," he remarked in his *Geography*.[13] Yet Strabo also added that he had no trustworthy witnesses for such an allegation, reinforcing the impression that the Romans and their supporters were interested only in denigrating the Celtic character and way of life.

This skepticism is strengthened by the fact that there are few references to human sacrifice in the ancient Irish sagas. There are certainly references to tributes, and to tributes on Samhain. In his *History of Ireland*, written in the seventeenth century, Geoffrey Keating noted that the Fomorians demanded milk, corn, and two-thirds of the newly born children from the ancient race of Neimheadh "on the eve of Samhain." But whether or not this tribute involved blood sacrifices is unclear.[14] First-born sacrifices are mentioned in a poem in the *Dindshenchas*, which records that children were sacrificed each Samhain to the idol *Cromm Crúaich* [the lord of the mound] at Mag Slécht in County Cavan.[15] But this may well have been embroidery, an embellishment by its Christian recorder that was intended to inflate the importance of St. Patrick, who is credited with eliminating such practices from Ireland. Human sacrifices are also noted in some of the folktales concerning the life of St. Columba, or Colm Cille, as he is known in Gaelic. In these stories there are references to a monk from Iona named Odran, a disciple of St. Patrick, who against the beliefs of his master offered himself in sacrifice to propitiate the demons that infested the isle of Iona, or to forestall famine, or, at St. Columba's request, to put down roots for a permanent Christian settlement in this part of Ireland. This evidence suggests that human sacrifice was customary at the dawn of the Christian age and indeed was not necessarily rejected as a form of divine appeasement by Christians themselves. Yet St. Patrick, in his own account of his campaign against pagan customs, makes no mention of human sacrifice at all.[16]

The fifth-century evidence about whether the Druids sacrificed humans is therefore highly ambiguous. Could it be that the Druids abandoned human sacrifice by then? Or could it be that the Druids had refrained from such rites all along, that the Romans simply projected their own past practices onto their enemies?

Two considerations should make us wary of believing that the Druids were peace-loving mystics who abhorred human sacrifice. Archeological remains reveal that the northern peoples of the Roman or pre-Roman era did sacrifice humans. The piles of heads at temple sites suggest that Celtic warriors kept the crania of their opponents as trophies and perhaps as offerings to the gods. The discovery of pits in the sanctuary floor of an Irish site on the hill of Tara in County Meath, all filled with the bones of animals and humans, also suggest sacrificial rites. The more recent excavations of bog men in Denmark and Britain point in the same direction. In the case of the "Lindow Man," the body found on Lindow Moss south of Manchester in 1984, the victim appeared to have been struck from behind, garrotted, and bled as he was dropped into the bog. It is, of course, conjecture as to whether or not this was a ritual sacrifice, let alone a sacrifice that likely occurred at a Celtic festival, but the suggestion that human sacrifice was part of the culture of the ancient "British" peoples cannot be easily dismissed.[17]

The second factor that must be taken into account revolves around the status of the early Irish sagas as historical evidence. These sagas were part of a long vernacular tradition that was written down centuries later and probably in corrupted and abbreviated form. These stories should be read as clues to the mystery of ancient lore and to the art of story-telling rather than as straightforward evidence of social practice. It is difficult to see how one can write a literal history of ancient Celtic peoples from these sources. Thus, it is dangerous to infer that no sacrifices took place because the Irish myths made little reference to them. The Romans may well have embellished their accounts of the sacrificial rites of their enemies, but their accounts cannot be discounted altogether. Nor, as historian Stuart Piggot has observed, can the Druids be exculpated from participating in them.[18] As the wise men of ancient Celtic societies, the Druidic priests very likely played an important role in appeasing the gods. The depiction of them as peace-loving bards is really an eighteenth- and nineteenth-century invention.

None of this evidence conclusively establishes Samhain as a peculiarly sanguinary festival, whatever Hollywood has subsequently made of it. One can speculate that human sacrifices were common to all quarterly Celtic festivals, Samhain included. But the sanguinary aspect of Samhain more frequently involved the annual slaughter of animals to reduce the livestock in the lean winter months rather than the ritual killing of humans, whether criminals, as Julius Caesar surmised, or first-born children, or tribal enemies.

In fact, the pagan origins of Halloween generally flow not from this sacrificial evidence but from a different set of symbolic practices. These revolve around the notion of Samhain as a festival of the dead and as a time of supernatural intensity heralding the onset of winter.

The notion that Samhain was a festival of the dead was first popularized by Sir James Frazer in the now classic *Golden Bough* (1890). He wrote that "the night which marks the transition from autumn to winter seems to have been of old the time of year when the souls of the departed were supposed to revisit their old homes in order to warm themselves by the fire and to comfort themselves with the good cheer provided from them in the kitchen or the parlour by their affectionate kinfolk."[19] This anachronistic description of a Celtic festival should make us wary, for it seems probable that Frazer confused the rites associated with All Souls' Day with those that preceded it.

In fact, there is no hard evidence that Samhain was specifically devoted to the dead or to ancestor worship, despite claims to the contrary by some American folklorists, some of whom have presumed that the feast was devoted to *Saman*, god of the dead.[20] Certainly, the feast was linked to the mythical peoples of Ireland. According to the ancient sagas, Samhain was the time when tribal peoples paid tribute to their conquerors and when the *sídh* might reveal the magnificent palaces of the gods of the underworld.[21] Insofar as Samhain was dedicated to anyone—and this is extremely conjectural—it appears to have been associated with the principal god of the Old Irish tradition, Eochaid Ollathaír, sometimes referred to as Dagda, who in *Tochmarc Etaíne*, or the *Wooing of Etaín*, had ritual intercourse with three divinities, including Mórrígan, the raven-goddess of war and fertility. Among other things, this coupling protected the crops.[22] This would make sense, since pastoral communities were likely anxious about their ability to survive the winter months with their available food supplies, especially when they had to bear the burden of quartering warriors within their compounds.

In marking the onset of winter, Samhain was closely associated with darkness and the supernatural. In Celtic lore, winter was the dark time of the year when "nature is asleep, summer has returned to the underworld, and the earth is desolate and inhospitable."[23] In Cornwall and Brittany, November was known as the dark or black month, the first of winter; in Scotland, it was called "*an Dudlachd*" or "gloom." Samhain was a time of divine couplings and dark omens, a time when malignant birds emerged from the caves of Crogham to prey upon mankind, led by one monstrous three-headed vulture whose foul breath withered the crops.[24]

As night overwhelmed day, so the supernatural abounded. In Ireland, the *fé-fiada*, the magic fog that rendered people invisible, was lifted on Samhain, and elves emerged from the fairy raths, erasing the boundaries between the real and otherworld. In the Irish saga the *Book of Lismore*, Fingein was visited every Samhain by a banshee, a fairy-woman, "who would relate to him all the marvels and precious things in all the royal strongholds of Ireland."[25] In the long nights of impending winter, the festival was closely related with prophecy and story-telling. It is no accident that many of the mythic events in the ancient sagas happened during this period. Mythic kings and heroes died on Samhain, and carousing Ulster warriors, the *Uliad*, met their death by fire and the sword at the hands of their Munster enemies. Samhain was also the occasion when the Formorians exacted tributes of grain, milk, and live children from their subordinates and when malevolent gods strove unsuccessfully to burn Tara, the meeting place of the five Irish provinces. Not all stories, of course, spoke of war and destruction. Some dealt with the prospect of rebirth and the triumph of true love, including the tale of Oenghus and Caer, the prince of love and the princess of the sídh, who fall in love despite parental disapproval and fly away as swans.[26]

What was especially noteworthy about Samhain was its status as a borderline festival. It took place between the autumn equinox and the winter solstice. In Celtic lore, it marked the boundary between summer and winter, light and darkness. In this respect, Samhain can be seen as a threshold, or what anthropologists would call a liminal festival.[27] It was a moment of ritual transition and altered states. It represented a time out of time, a brief interval "when the normal order of the universe is suspended" and "charged with a peculiar preternatural energy."[28] These qualities would continue to resonate through the celebration of Halloween.

❦ 2 ❦

FESTIVE RITES
Halloween in the British Isles

If Samhain imparted to Halloween a supernatural charge and an intrinsic liminality, it did not offer much in the way of actual ritual practices, save in its fire rites. Most of these developed in conjunction with the medieval holy days of All Souls' and All Saints' Day. Within the history of Christian festivals, these holidays were comparatively late arrivals. Initially, the early Christians celebrated those martyred by the pagan emperors rather than the saints. In the fourth century this commemoration occurred on 13 May, but in the next century the observances of different churches diverged, with the Syrian churches holding their festival of the martyrs during Easter week and the Greeks on the Sunday after Pentecost, leaving only the Romans to hold to the original day in May. Festivals commemorating the saints as opposed to the original Christian martyrs appear to have been observed by 800. In England and Germany, this celebration took place on 1 November. In Ireland, it was commemorated on 20 April, a chronology that contradicts the widely held view that the November date was chosen to Christianize the festival of Samhain.

The festival honoring all souls was largely the inspiration of the Cluniacs, the French monastic order, although the Spanish churches were probably the first to develop such a holy day, since they commemorated the "faithfully departed" on Pentecost Monday as early as 650. Almost 250 years later, in 998, the abbot of Cluny, Odilo, ordered a solemn mass for the souls of the Christian dead in his monastery and its affiliated houses. The date Odilo chose was in February, but over the course of the next two centuries, the commemoration was moved to the day after All Saints' on the grounds that saints could be important intercessors for departed souls facing divine judgment. By the end of the twelfth century, the linked festivals of All Saints' and All Souls', Todos Santos or Tots Sants in Spanish, or Hallowtide in English, were well-established liturgical moments in the Christian year. At the end of the Middle Ages they were among the most important. The feast of All Saints' and All Souls' was one of the six days of obligation, marked by high masses and prayers. It was a holiday that affirmed the collective claims that the dead had on the living. Its requiem masses also served as insurance against hauntings, for ghosts were generally "understood to be dead relatives who visited their kin to rectify wrongs committed against them while alive and to enforce the obligations of kinship."[1] As night fell and All Souls' Day arrived, bells were also rung for the souls in purgatory. These were people who were in a spiritual suspension, in an intermediary space between heaven and hell, for whom prayers and penance could be made for their sins before the day of judgment. In preparation for Hallowtide, churches made sure that their bells were in good shape, for in some places they were rung all night to ward off demonic spirits. In the churchwardens' accounts of Heybridge in Essex in 1517, for example, there were payments to Andrew Elyott and John Gidney of Maldon to repair the "bell knappelle" and rope for "Hallowmasse."[2]

These were the basic church rituals associated with Hallowtide, but over time other customs were added. In Naples, the charnel houses containing the bones of the dead were opened on All Souls' Day and decorated with flowers. Crowds thronged through them to visit the bodies of their friends and relatives. Sometimes the cadavers were dressed in robes and placed in niches along the walls. In Brittany, the clergy led a solemn procession to the graveyard, where the local people would consecrate the graves of their kin with holy water or milk. At Salerno, and indeed elsewhere in Catholic Europe, household members would lay out food for the dead, whose souls were expected to return to their former abodes on All Souls' Day. As we see in chapter 7, this practice has obvious links to the current rituals of the Mexican Day of the Dead, notably to the meticulously prepared *ofrendas*, or family altars.[3]

In England, many churches purchased extra candles or torches for the ecclesiastical processions of Hallowtide. Bonfires were also built in graveyards to ward off malevolent spirits. At one rich parish in London, St. Mary Woolnoth, five young garlanded women were hired in 1539 to play harps by lamplight.[4] In Bristol, then a burgeoning Atlantic port, the mayor was expected to entertain the city council before Hallowmass with "fires and their drinkings with spiced cakebread and sundry wines." In fact, it became customary in many towns and villages for the richer parishioners to offer doles to the poor during Hallowtide in return for prayers to the dead, emulating the medieval custom of the well-to-do, who left small bequests for this purpose to parishes or chantries. The spectacle of the poor receiving food for prayers at Hallowtide was well established by Shakespeare's day. In his comedy *Two Gentlemen of Verona*, Speed mockingly accuses his master of "puling [whining or whimpering], like a beggar at Hallowmas."[5]

All Saints' and All Souls' Day were also times with a special significance to children and young adults, a matter of some importance in the light of Halloween's subsequent evolution. To prepare for winter, the slaughter of livestock conventionally began in earnest on All Saints' Day. As one sixteenth-century tract put it: "At Hallontide slaughter time entereth in."[6] This was a boon to local lads. The dead animals provided bladders that could be used for ball games, inaugurating the beginning of the football season when rival villages, or rival ends of the same village, would try to rough and tumble their way to victory.

Hallowtide was also sporty in a different context, one associated with marriages and masking. All Saints' not only honored the saints and martyrs of the church, but its liturgy also referred to "the wise virgins awaiting the coming of the bridegroom," thereby anticipating forthcoming marriages and a replenishing of the Christian flock. Because this injunction to marry was also sung by choristers with their hoods up "in the manner of virgin women," it also introduced the season of masking and impersonation that by then characterized the November and Christmas calendar.[7] In this season of misrule, choristers became boy bishops and urban leaders were temporarily usurped from power by mock-mayors and sheriffs in a ritualized topsy-turvy world replete with "subtle disguisings, masks, and mummeries."[8] In country districts, "the wilde heades of the parish" chose a "Ground Capitaine [grand captain] of mischeef whom they innoble with the title of my Lorde of Misserule," Philip Stubbs observed. Gaudily attired with ribbons, bells, and handkerchiefs "borrowed for the most parte of their prettie Mopsies," this merry troupe of revelers paraded the churchyards with "their Hobby horses and other monsters shirmishyng amongst the throng," singing and dancing "with such a confused noise that no man can heare his own voice." These mummers demanded tributes from the neighborhood to maintain their "Heathenerie, Devilrie," and "Drunkennesse," Stubbs continued. Those that refused to contribute were "mocked and flouted at shamefully, yea, and many times carried upon the cowlstaff, and dived head and ears in water, and otherwise most horribly abused."[9] Consequently, Hallowtide was closely associated with the role reversals and shaming rituals—rough music, skimmingtons, charivari—that became an integral part of early modern popular culture.[10] Indeed, at Hallowtide in 1631, in a small village called Chêne near Geneva, Besançon Daussy was subjected to a humiliating charivari for allowing his wife to abuse him. In the eyes of his neighbors, he had abrogated his role as the head of his household. According to the reports that reached the authorities in Geneva, he was placed backward on a horse and led around the marketplace with his hands clutching the tail while an impersonator of his spouse struck him with a distaff. Later, when he complained to the authorities about his mistreatment, his house was stoned, his vines were cut, and his cow was sold. The organizers of the charivari, resenting his appeal to outsiders, also defamed Daussy and his wife with cries of "bougre" [bogey] and "sorcier" [witch].[11]

Hallowtide was thus one of those occasions when flagrant violations of community norms might be addressed. It was a time when choristers would cross-dress and begin the revels that culminated in the Christmas Feast of Fools, normally reserved for 28 December, the Feast of the Holy Innocents. It was a time when youths rang bells for their dead ancestors and extended their misrule into the streets.[12] As one poet put it: "How fit our well-rank'd Feasts do follow/All mischief comes after All-Hallow."[13] In less formal settings, it was a time when the young men of the village would ring in the winter season, play the fool, gang together to play football, and perhaps, under cover of that collective, carry out some rough justice against unpopular neighbors.

Yet in the early modern era, at least, the retributive or carnivalesque qualities of Hallowtide were counterbalanced by the solemn task of

An eighteenth-century skimmington or charivari, by William Hogarth, for Samuel Butler's *Hudibras* series, 1726.

honoring the dead. All Souls' was often marked by reverence rather than profanity. It was quintessentially a day for honoring the dead, with midnight vigils at gravesites and, until the eighteenth century, domestic offerings of food and clothing for the recently departed. As late as a century ago in Catholic Ireland, it was commonly believed that the dead would return on All Hallow Eve or on the days thereafter. In New-market, County Cork, the "woman of the house" would light candles and leave spring water for the deceased visitors.[14]

In England, the rituals of Hallowtide came under attack during the Reformation of the sixteenth century. Protestants denounced purgatory as a popish doctrine incompatible with the notion of predestination. They deplored the idea that the living could influence the condition of the dead through their prayers and rejected the belief that the saints could function as intermediaries between humans and Christ. Determined to eliminate all rituals that upheld such a notion, Arch-bishop Thomas Cranmer attempted to abolish the ringing of bells for the dead in 1546. But Henry VIII refused to sign the edict, believing it might jeopardize a potential rapprochement with France and the Holy Roman Empire. His more Protestant son, Edward VI, had fewer reservations. His royal commissions successfully enforced a ban in 1548, with only a few parishes defying the injunction. The rituals of Hallow-mass were revived briefly under his Catholic successor, Mary, but they were checked once more under Elizabeth I, when the services com-memorating the dead were dropped from the litany of 1559. All Saints' Day was retained, but as an occasion to celebrate the saints as out-standing Christians, not as semi-divine intercessors.

It proved more difficult for the Anglican Church to eliminate the devotions to the dead than to eliminate other Catholic practices, because some of them could be practiced without clerical guidance or ornaments. In North Wales, candelit processions persisted; in England, bells continued to be rung. People were brought before the church courts for ringing bells on All Saints' Night throughout the 1560s and the custom was still being condemned twenty years later, especially in

Ripon in the North Riding of Yorkshire, where several clergymen were prosecuted for attempting to revive the holiday.[15] In more remote areas of the country, Hallowtide nonetheless survived for a few more decades in England. In Wellington, Somerset, in 1604, revelers attacked a constable who attempted to suppress the customary festivities.[16]

By the end of Elizabeth's reign, the official practices surrounding Hallowmass had been eliminated. Yet the more popular customs associated with the holiday did survive in some areas. According to the *Gentleman's Magazine* for 1783, Catholics continued to light fires on hilltops on All Saints' Night.[17] In the more remote areas of the Pennines there were torchlight ceremonies to commemorate the dead. At Whalley, in Lancashire, near the forest of Pendle, families formed a circle and prayed for the souls of the departed until the flames burned out. Similar Hallowtide rituals were observed in the Derbyshire village of Findern, on the moors of Marton, and in the hills surrounding the Fylde, sometimes on sites known as "Purgatory field" or "Purgatory farm." The rite itself was known as "Teanlay," a word likely derived from the Old English *tendan*, meaning to kindle, and may well have fused the customs of Hallowmass with older fire rituals of protection and purification noted by Sir James Frazer and others. It was reported, for instance, that the farmers in Fylde would circle their fields "with a burning wisp of straw at the point of a fork" to protect the crop from weeds.[18]

Alongside these fire rituals was the more extensive practice of "souling." The custom of baking bread or soul cakes for "all crysten [christened] souls" was well established before the Reformation. This food was conventionally distributed to all relatives and poor neighbors who offered to pray for the souls in purgatory, underscoring the belief that prayers and ritual practices could smooth or speed a soul's passage to heaven.[19] This custom was likely revived or revamped by Catholics as a popular response to the elimination of All Souls' Day from the official religious calendar by the Protestants. The antiquary John Aubrey noted its popularity in seventeenth-century Shropshire. "There is sett on the Board a high-heap of Soule-cakes," he remarked, "lyeing one upon another like the picture of the Sew-Bread in the old Bibles. They are about the bignesse of 2d [tuppenny] cakes and nearly all the visitants that day take one," upon reciting the rhyme,

> A Soule-cake, a Soule-cake,
> Have mercy on all Christian soules for a soule-cake.[20]

Souling is important to our investigation of Halloween in two respects. First, the rituals surrounding souling, in which supplicants moved from door to door asking for food in return for a prayer for the dead, bear a resemblance to modern Halloween customs, especially since soulers went from house to house with hollowed-out turnip lanterns, whose candle connoted a soul trapped in purgatory. In other words, with what we might describe as mobile jack-o'-lanterns.

Second, souling customs offer a clue to the survival of Hallowmass in England after the Protestant Reformation. It is a tricky one, since the historian is heavily reliant upon the researches of nineteenth-century folklorists for his or her evidence. One has to engage in what must be a retrospective reading of the rite. But there does seem to be some concordance between the continued observance of the custom and areas noted for their recusancy, that is, for the survival of Catholicism after the Protestant Reformation. These included the counties of Yorkshire, Lancashire, Cheshire, Shropshire, Staffordshire, and the peak district of Derbyshire. The concordance is not exact. There were areas of recusancy in the south of England, most notably in Hampshire and Sussex, where souling does not appear to have survived or even practiced. In contrast, souling was observed in parts of Wales, most notably in Monmouth and Caenarvonshire, and even as far south as Herefordshire and Somerset, even though these areas were not noted for their Catholicism.

The discrepancy may be explained by the fact that souling remained an important occasion for soliciting food and money from rich neighbors during the bleak winter months. "Cold winter it is coming on, dark, dirty, wet and cold," ran one Cheshire souling song, "To try your good nature, this night we do make bold." Or as one souling patter from Somersetshire put it: "My clothes are very ragged/My shoes are very thin/I've got a little pocket/To put three halfpence in/And I'll never come a souling/Till another year."[21] As these rhymes suggest, souling was often only nominally concerned with praying for souls in purgatory. It formed part of a ritual cycle of enforced charity by the laboring classes as winter set in. As such, it was but one of many possible occasions for door-to-door treating. There were other "doleing days" that could suit: Guy Fawkes Day (5 November); St. Clement's Day (23 November); St. Catherine's Day (25 November); St. Andrew's Day (30 November); even St. Nicholas's Day (6 December) and St. Thomas's (21 December), just a few days before Christmas.[22] Which day was chosen would depend upon a variety of factors: the local agrarian cycle, the religious legacy of the region, or the patronage of particular saints by industrial trades. St. Catherine was the patron saint of the Kentish ropemakers, for instance, and of the Buckinghamshire lacemakers; St. Clement of the blacksmiths, anchor-makers, and more generally of the naval dockyards.

Souling survived in northern England, especially in Lancashire and Cheshire. In the latter, All Souls' Day even featured a mummer's play in which a hobby horse would remonstrate with mean-spirited neighbors. "From All Souls' Day to Christmas Day," noted one journal in 1850, "Old Hob is carried about; this consists of a horse's head enveloped in a sheet, taken from door to door, accompanied by the singing of doggerel-begging rhymes."[23] But souling faced increasing competition from other doleing days in the West Midlands and was more or less subsumed by them in the South,[24] a pattern that appears to confirm the idea that Hallowtide customs survived principally in Catholic areas distant from London, in areas where official vigilance was weak.

If many of the religious customs associated with All Hallows and All Souls had died out by the middle of the seventeenth century, it is

Seeing spirits in the air, woodcut by Joseph Glanville, 1700.

nonetheless clear the days were still regarded as a time of supernatural intensity. On Halloween, as it came to be known in the eighteenth century, ghosts, spirits, and witches were likely to be abroad. Samuel Bamford, a radical agitator of the early nineteenth century, and one who was reared in the Protestant religion, recalled that the two nights of All Saints' and All Souls' were "especially set apart for spiritual appearances." In his hometown of Middleton in Lancashire, it was popularly believed that "the spirits of all those who should die" in the following year would appear in "bodily shape" on these ghoulish nights.[25] In other parts of the county, there was even a custom of "Lating" or "Leeting [Scaring or Driving Out] the Witches," of burning candles or torches to ward off evil spirits. Sometimes these candles were carried about the hills during the hour before midnight. If the candle continued to burn during this "witching hour," then the carrier would enjoy an immunity from witches for the coming year.[26]

The survival of these beliefs suggests that Halloween continued to be an important time for divinations or omens in England, even when the association of souling customs to purgatory had weakened.[27] A woman born on Halloween was thought to have supernatural powers, an unusual capacity to foretell the future, especially with regard to her own family. Even people born on another day believed they could predict a harsh or mild winter by the prevailing winds on Halloween. People could also learn of the impending deaths of neighbors from the shadowy shapes in the churchyard, or if they glimpsed a coffin while riddling corn in a barn. Death was also to be expected if one dropped egg white into a glass of water and detected a shroud.[28]

Not all of the fortune-telling rituals of Halloween were so lugubrious, of course. All Hallows had been associated with marriage as well as death, and consequently many of the divinations were rather more upbeat. In Derbyshire, young women customarily placed a sprig of rosemary or a crooked sixpence under their pillow on Halloween in order to dream of their future husbands. In Worcestershire, young women threw a ball of new worsted wool through an open window at midnight. Whoever picked up the worsted and whispered his name would be her future spouse. In Cornwall, the trade or profession of a husband could be divined by running molten lead through cold water. Halloween was also a time when the fidelity of lovers could be tested or the prospect of marriage foretold by the way nuts popped in the fire. If the nuts stayed together, the love-match would prosper; if they flew apart, so, too, would the lovers."[29]

Thus, Halloween in England continued to be associated with the supernatural, but after the Reformation there was no common set of ritual practices marking the event. If there was one autumnal holiday

Divining the future on Halloween from three bowls or "luggies." From an 1811 Edinburgh edition of Robert Burns, *Poems*.

that achieved national status in England, it was the anniversary of the discovery of the Gunpowder Plot of 1605. This was the abortive attempt by a group of Catholic malcontents, led by Guy Fawkes, to blow up the houses of Parliament. In the course of the seventeenth and eighteenth centuries, the Gunpowder Plot became an integral part of the calendar of national commemoration in England, legitimized by Parliament and included in the Book of Common Prayer until 1859. This holiday symbolized England's deliverance from the Catholic menace. After 1688, it acquired a double meaning, for it also represented the nation's deliverance from the Catholicizing and potentially absolutist monarchy of King James II. It was on the Fifth of November that William of Orange landed at Torbay to contest the throne in the name of Protestantism and parliamentary liberty.

During the first half of the eighteenth century, the Fifth of November had a partisan political flavor, privileging Whig over Tory ideologies. By the 1760s, it was a festival that was firmly embedded in popular politics as a day of national deliverance from Catholicism and absolutist rule, one that was critical to the shaping of national identities in opposition to Britain's most powerful neighbor and imperial rival, France. Popularly known as Guy Fawkes or Bonfire Night, the Fifth of November became the occasion for roasting in effigy the Catholic conspirator Guy Fawkes or his master, the Pope, or for that matter any unpopular politician, clergyman, or magistrate whose actions seemed authoritarian or arbitrary. In 1820, the inhabitants of Guisborough in Yorkshire used the holiday to signal their displeasure at George IV's mean-spirited, inquisitorial policy toward his estranged wife, Queen Caroline. During the Crimean War, the Emperor of Russia was burnt in effigy in villages in Leicestershire.[30] In Lewes, Sussex, where the vitality of Guy Fawkes Day was and is still sustained by local bonfire societies, inhabitants would be regularly treated to the rants of mock-priests decrying the latest public scandal.[31]

Although Bonfire Night lost some of its political edge after the 1850s, it continued to be a rowdy, raucous festival. It featured festive tributes from neighbors and the foraging for winter fuel on a conspicuous scale. In the North Riding of Yorkshire, people would stroll around the villages collecting money for the tar barrels that were used to fuel the bonfire, and "if no money was given them, they would lay hands on besoms, wood, sticks or anything else likely to be of use for the bonfire." In Oxfordshire, it was "considered quite lawful to appropriate any old wood" that could be found for the bonfire.[32] The notion that the customary festive license of the holiday put revelers beyond the law was also to be found in Leicestershire. In the early nineteenth century, when there was a continuing war between the landed gentry and the country population over the rights to hunt wild game, the Fifth of November was a time when local poachers felt they had a right to trap rabbits and shoot partridges with impunity.[33]

If Bonfire Night was sometimes an occasion when community justice was served, it was invariably a night of high spirits and pranks. The London radical Francis Place thought the holiday a blackguard festival, when the rougher elements of the community dominated the streets and when unpopular individuals ran the risk of being "guyed" or hazed for their censorious or niggardly behavior. "The Guy was made up of old cloaths stuffed with hay and straw," Place recalled,

> the head was usually an old barber's block with a mask for a face, it was seated on an old chair, and was carried in the same manner by two boys. A number of boys went in front, another party behind, and two or three on each side, they were all armed with bludgeons. The strongest or most valiant of the boys carried the begging box in the front and led the way.[34]

Even outside the capital, the streets were often filled with revelers bent on mischief on Bonfire Night. In Yorkshire, gangs of youths ranged the streets, striking doors with bags of stones and shouting out, "Fift' o' November, we'll mak' ye' remember." Because of the uproarious

PROCESSION OF A GUY.

Parading the guy on Bonfire Night, a nineteenth-century burlesque from Robert Chambers, *The Book of Days* (1888).

atmosphere and prattle it provoked, the festival was popularly known as "Babblin' Neet."[35] At Guildford, in Surrey, the festivities frequently got out of hand. In 1851, Henry Peak remembered seeing "a great fire burning" in the town.

> Every shop window . . . was barricaded; and wet straw and manure heaped [up] to prevent the penetration of fireworks; . . . these being immense squibs . . . 12 or 15 inches . . . being chiefly loaded with gunpowder . . . curiosity drew me towards the fire, where a lawless crowd was

gathered; the chiefs, fantastically dressed, were the "Guys" Society . . . who gave orders to the mob by means of a horn [whose] blasts were understood and acted upon.[36]

In subsequent decades, local magistrates and elites, backed by friendly and temperance societies, tried to bring these festivities to some kind of order. When the police superintendent of Market Harborough attempted to ban the burning of tar barrels on Guy Fawkes Night in 1874, he was forced to take refuge in a local hotel and had the humiliation of seeing his own effigy burned in tar barrels the following day. According to local reports, the band that led the protest played a popular opera song entitled, "We'll run him in."[37]

As a night of high spirits and youthful rascality, and as a ritual of social reversal, Guy Fawkes Night eclipsed Halloween in England, as it would in Australia and New Zealand, where it was sometimes called Danger or Mischievous Night.[38] Given the close proximity of the festivals, which fell within five days of one another, it was predictable that some of the souling rituals of Halloween would spill over to the Fifth of November. In Southrepps and other places in Norfolk, the turnip lanterns that traditionally symbolized souls in purgatory were much in evidence on Bonfire Night. In Lincolnshire, some of the fire rituals commonly associated with Halloween were transferred to the Fifth of November. Celebrants threw stones into the bonfire and on the following morning discerned their future from the way they were placed. In Yorkshire, Lancashire, and Derbyshire, thar cakes or parkins, usually made out of treacle and oatmeal, formed part of the festive fare. These were clearly reminiscent of the soul cakes distributed at Hallowtide, even though they were made of sweeter and heavier ingredients.

Guy Fawkes Night was a quintessentially English festival that achieved national significance before the union with either Scotland or Ireland. In Scotland, the anniversary also became a day of national thanksgiving, as in England. Together with the anniversary of King

James's deliverance from the Gowrie conspiracy in 1600, the Fifth of November formed part of a providential Protestant calendar that both helped construct a Scottish national identity. In Edinburgh and other Scottish cities, bonfires were a familiar site on the Fifth, and continued to be so after the political significance of the anniversary declined in importance. In 1905, William Anderson, then a coalman in Edinburgh, remarked that there were "still a lot of Guy's going about."[39]

What was different about the Scottish celebration of Bonfire Night was its compatibility with Halloween. There is no evidence that the state-sponsored Fifth displaced or radically altered the conventions of Halloween, despite the fact that the Kirk strove to ban saints' days that smacked of "popery." This was because the Scottish Kirk took a pragmatic attitude toward seasonal revels that were important to the life cycle and rites of passage of local communities, especially where it anticipated real difficulty in curbing them.[40] The result was that Halloween continued to coexist and indeed vie with the Fifth of November as a night of prankish fun. In the twentieth century, boosted no doubt by Burn's merry verses on Halloween and his stature as a national poet, the eve of All Souls' was often considered the more quintessentially Scottish of the two festivals.[41] "What can you Englishers . . . ken o' Hallowe'en," asks John Galt's Mungo Affleck, in a novel set in the seventeenth century but written in 1823. "O, sir, Hallowe'en among us is a dreadful night! witches and warlocks, and a'lang-nebbit things, hae a power and dominion unspeakable on Hallowe'en."[42] Even when the fearful superstition of witches and warlocks lost much of its credibility, masking continued. Although the media made little of it, "guising" on Halloween, dressing up and doing a turn at the neighbors' houses, was integral to the Scottish festive cycle as late as the 1950s and 1960s.[43]

In Ireland, where a Protestant minority presided over a Catholic population, Guy Fawkes Day was predictably more contentious. In the eighteenth century, the Fifth of November was occasionally observed as a public holiday at which church bells were rung and civic dinners held. But it was conventionally eclipsed by 4 November, the birthday of William of Orange, the English monarch who defeated the Jacobite army in Ireland during the 1690s and reestablished Protestant rule in that country. The Fourth of November was a day when troops and volunteers would parade the streets and when the preeminently Protestant Boyne and Enniskillen societies would celebrate the day with dinners and bonfires. It was also celebrated as the anniversary of William's landing in England in 1688. It was only after Catholic emancipation (1828), as the sectarian politics of Ireland heated up, that the Fifth of November began to be commemorated vigorously by Orangemen.[44] To this day, Guy Fawkes Night is still observed in parts of Northern Ireland, where it remains a controversial symbol of sectarian identity.[45]

Despite its obvious Orange referent, the Fifth of November never achieved the status of the Twelfth of July, the Orange anniversary of the Battles of the Boyne and Aughrim, nor of the Protestant defense of Londonderry. Consequently, it did not supplant Halloween as the most important fall/winter festival. This was as true of Protestants as it was of Catholics, who would have inevitably identified the Fifth of November with the Protestant planter minority and the Williamite suppression of Ireland. Over the years, some of the Bonfire Night rituals, in particular, fireworks and effigy-burnings, were transferred to Halloween in Northern Ireland.[46] If Bonfire Night appropriated some of the rites of Hallowtide in England, in Northern Ireland the appropriation has gone the other way.

In Ireland and Scotland, then, Halloween was largely untouched by the Protestant Reformation. If the Kirk found it politic to ignore Halloween rituals, so, too, did the Protestant Church of Ireland, which was more concerned with curbing Catholic priests and policing the declining rump of Catholic landlords than worrying unduly about the popular superstitions of the peasantry. In fact, from the seventeenth century onward, the folklore associated with Halloween flourished without much church intervention, sometimes accenting and even rejuvenating older pagan customs. In the Scottish Highlands, Hallow fires blazed from cairns and hilltops. Their ashes were later placed in magical circles around which people danced. In some areas, there were torchlight processions around the fields to ensure their fertility or to ward off evil spirits or witches. Firebrands were also used to purify cattle at what was sometimes known as Ceitein Samhraidh, the first day of winter. Many of these customs recalled the fire rituals of Samhain that were to be found in the ancient Celtic sagas. The fires themselves were known as *samhnag* or *samhnagan* in many Gaelic-speaking areas.

In Ireland, too, where the oral traditions of Celtic practices were stronger, Halloween was often closely associated with Samhain. In West Limerick, Ardee, and Donegal, people born in the late nineteenth century continued to refer to Halloween as Oiche Samna or Shamna, or simply as Sean Saman or Samayn. The close association of Halloween with pagan Celtic practices meant that in some places the holiday was differentiated from All Souls'. The latter was a time of vigils for the dead, for whom food was prepared in a manner reminiscent of the Mexican Day of the Dead. As one inhabitant of Knocknagree, County Clare, declared, All Souls' was the night when "all who ever lived and died in any house were all allowed to visit."[47] Halloween, in contrast, was a time of foreboding and omens, when the raths of the countryside were held in "superstitious awe." In County Connaught and County Kildare, it was even known as *Puca* Night, a reference to the imps who purportedly befouled the fruit and crops still in the fields.[48] As one respondent observed: "the good people [fairies] were supposed to be very active on Hollantide night. People did not throw water or sweep out floors that night for fear of offending the good people."[49]

Yet the distinction between Halloween and All Souls' was by no means clear-cut, something underscored by the fact that Halloweve or Hollantide could be celebrated anywhere between 31 October and 2 November. The wandering spirits associated with ancient Samhain and the wandering souls of purgatory could be acknowledged at the same time, even by priests. On one Halloween, a Mitchelstown priest told his congregation that "they should drive slowly home, so as to give time to the souls roaming at this time to get out of the way."[50]

The syncretism or blending of Christian and pagan belief was also reflected in Scottish practice. The Halloween supper in Scotland, for instance, often featured a *sau'mas* (All Souls') loaf. But it could also feature a porridge known as *sowens*, phonetically the phrase for Samhain, or a three-cornered cake called bannock, in which was carved a design representing the rays of the sun. Highlanders no longer prayed for the dead on Halloween, but they did bless their fishing boats by marking them with a cross. On the isle of Lewis, the inhabitants made a malt sacrifice to a sea-god named Shony before repairing to St. Malvey's chapel for a moment's silence, and then to the fields for the evening's revels. Ministers on the island thought this too pagan a ceremony and successfully suppressed the custom in 1670, only to discover its reappearance on Maundy Thursday, at the opening of the fishing season.[51]

It is not always easy to track the development of Halloween in Ireland and Scotland from the mid-seventeenth century, largely because one has to trace ritual practices from folkloric evidence that do not necessarily reflect how the holiday might have changed; these rituals may not be "authentic" or "timeless" examples of preindustrial times. But three observations seem in order.

The first is that Halloween's mummery and misrule had a long and buoyant history, surviving into the twentieth century. In the Shetland Isles, *gruliks* or *skeklers*, young men dressed up in fantastic costumes made of animal skin or straw, went from house to house, dancing, singing, and begging for gifts. Similar conventions existed in Mulligar, in West Meath. As one witness told the Irish Folklore Commission of the 1940s,

> Young people sometimes dressed up in strange garments, the boys going as girls; the girls as old men or women with masks or faces, perhaps a bit of flour-bag or calico with slits

for eyes, nose and mouth, the beard and brows drawn with boot polish, window curtains or veils and the like. A little band of them goes from one neighbour to another—never far from home—one member may have a mouth-organ or the like, they go into the kitchen & dance a "half-set," play music and come out. They don't seek money or food, but if an apple were handed [them], they'd take it, or a few nuts.[52]

Not all visits to houses were so innocent. In the tradition of mummery, revelers used such occasions to play tricks upon neighbors and occasionally to mete out rough justice to the most unpopular. Mimicking the malignant spirits who were widely believed to be abroad on Halloween, gangs of youths blocked up chimneys, rampaged cabbage patches, battered doors, unhinged gates, and unstabled horses. In nineteenth-century Cromarty, revelers even sought out lone women whom they could haze as a witch. On the island of Coll, it was said that "great liberties are taken in the way of stealing and hiding articles belonging to other people." The same was said of Kilbeggan and Rathowen in Ireland. Here, local inhabitants admitted to the Folklore Commission of 1941/42 that there was often "considerable damage done."[53] If neighbors happened to incur the wrath of the community for some antisocial act, the retributions could be severe. In West Meath in Ireland, such retributions took the form of a ritual hazing, the culprit being burnt in effigy before his or her door.[54] More typically, they would involve attacks upon a person's property. "If an individual happened to be disliked in the place," observed one Scot in 1911, "he was sure to suffer dreadfully on these occasions. His doors would be broken, and frequently not a cabbage left standing in his garden."[55] Such was Halloween's reputation as a night of festive retribution that in some parts of Scotland the imperatives of community justice prevailed over private property, to a point that the Kirk-session found it impossible to enforce law and order.

The conventions of misrule gave young males a prescribed role in

Halloween, although it was clearly open to abuse. It was their job to solicit peat and collect wood and fern for the bonfires. In Skye it was reported that they exercised "great licence, taking barrels, even doors, wheelbarrows and carts" for the communal bonfire,[56] presumably with some reckoning of what each household should contribute. Here, and in the guising and mischief that accompanied the night, male youths were clearly the dispensers of rough justice in their communities and their unofficial spokesmen.

Although young women were sometimes masked on Halloween, the holiday was indisputably an important occasion for male bonding among revelers. The activities that took place within and near the home, however, tended to focus upon the aspirations of young women. Apart from the games such as apple-bobbing that were played on Halloween by all members of the family, Halloween acquired a special significance as a courtship ritual or augury for marriage. The way stones settled in bonfires, the way nuts cracked in the heat, the shape of kale stalks pulled from the ground, the people or sounds one encountered at the midnight hour at a crossroads or stile—all were windows to the future. Some of these rites foretold forthcoming deaths, a predictable message in view of the holiday's long association with the dying, and one that in Ireland persisted in the aftermath of the potato famine of the mid-nineteenth century. But where killer epidemics declined in potency and the demographic fortunes of young people began to improve, as least after infancy, the spells and omens of Halloween increasingly focused upon future marriage prospects: who, when, whether one would marry; whether one's partner would be handsome or faithful or chaste at marriage. As the lawyer and agriculturalist William Aiton remarked of Halloween in Ayrshire at the turn of the nineteenth century, "many spells were then used to discover matters of futurity; particularly respecting marriages. Many of the lower orders, in that country still believe the devil is ready at their call, and on their using certain capers and spells to discover a secret which generally occupies much of their thought; namely, who is to be their future spouse."[57]

These divinations were part of the mating process in a fundamentally homosocial world, where men and women tended to work and play in gender-distinct spheres, to a far greater extent than today. It was in the larger festive settings that young men and women contemplated their marriage prospects and in public view consolidated or broke off courtships. Halloween was one such setting. Fortune-telling rituals and the public courting that accompanied it were associated with a string of holidays, including St. Agnes' Eve (20 January) Valentine's Day, St. David's Day (1 March), May Day (1 May), and St. Faith's Day (6 October).[58] But rather than being associated predominantly with death and the undead (those in purgatory), Halloween became one of those occasions in the ritual year when young adolescents tried to channel their sexuality into more permanent unions. As the *Gentleman's Magazine* remarked as early as 1784 of one of the dominant domestic rituals of Halloween, one that gave rise to the popular metonym of Nut-crack Night:

> The young folks amuse themselves with *burning nuts in pairs* on the bar of the grate, or among the warm embers, to which they give their name and that of their lovers, or those of their friends who are supposed to have such attachments, and from the manner of their burning and duration of the flame, draw such inferences respecting the constancy or strength of their passions, as usually promote mirth and good humour.[59]

As one observer from Ballygoblin, County Cork, explained to the Irish Folklore Commission, divinatory games were played by "young people anxious about marriage prospects."[60] This helps explain the popularity of Robert Burn's *Halloween* as a critical referent of the holiday. This poem is essentially a burlesque account of Halloween's games and divinations among the Ayrshire peasantry of the late eighteenth century, with the accent firmly upon future marriages than forebodings of death.

Courting on Halloween, from a London and New York edition of Robert
Burns, *Poetical Works*, 1856.

It is one of spells gone awry, of wishful couplings and disappointed hopes. In the case of Rab and Nelly, whose "tap-pickle maist was lost,/When kiutlan in the Fause-house/Wi' him that night," it also recalled lovemaking in the corn and the loss of virginity.[61]

By the eighteenth century, then, Halloween's superstitions were being translated into courtship rituals and games. They were being adapted to a more secular milieu in which expectations of life were increasing. The shift of emphasis can be seen in the adaptation of the medieval *memento mori* to Halloween. A *memento mori* is a reminder or foreboding of death, captured in medieval woodcuts in the shape of a skull, an hourglass, a coffin, or a skeleton. In the translation of this convention to Halloween, when young women divine their fate at the midnight hour, the visage encountered is more likely to be her future husband than the mask of death. Only rarely do the divination rituals mention a coffin or a ghost, or, in the case of a women of Lewis divining in a grain-drying kiln, the voice of the Grim Reaper.[62] Halloween in Britain increasingly celebrated life, not death. The link to Hallowtide, to the older conventions of All Saints and All Souls, was becoming less specific. The link pertained largely to the supernatural, reinforcing earlier folkloric associations with Samhain. Save in the most Catholic of areas, it no longer addressed souls trapped in purgatory and the need for intercessory prayer.

Yet there were some elements of continuity in the way Halloween was perceived. The holiday continued to be associated with the changing seasons, with the ending of summer and the triumph of night over day. "At Hallowmass, whan nights grown lang," wrote the eighteenth-century Scottish poet, Robert Fergusson, "And *starnies* [stars] shine fu' clear,/Whan fock, the nippin cald to bang [When folk the nipping cold overcome], Their winter *hap-warms* [wraps, overcoats] wear."[63] Nearly two centuries, later a man from County Wexford observed that "'All Holland' was looked on as the great parting of the ways—the 'suns' of summer and 'mellows' of autumn had, so to speak, come to a standstill and the festival of 'All Holland' filled the intervening time-space between them and the cold icy grip of winter."[64]

Within the agricultural cycle, Halloween was traditionally a time for renewing leases; hiring laborers; rethatching cottages; gathering crops, nuts, fruit, and peat; and slaughtering animals. In the corn-growing areas of Britain, it followed hard on the ritualized cutting of the cailleach, the "hag," or last sheaf. Accordingly, the Halloween supper was often a harvest supper featuring grain or fruit-based items, especially those associated with the potato: champ (mashed potatoes with milk, butter, and leeks), colcannon (mashed potatoes with cabbage), or boxty (fried colcannon).[65] Some of the divinatory practices and games associated with Halloween also stemmed from its place in the agricultural cycle. Finding rings hidden in colcannon (an augury of marriage); reading the shapes of apple peels to divine the first letter of a future spouse's name; burning nuts at the fireside to discover whether courtships would progress to the altar—all these practices, and those relating to the scattering of hemp seed or corn, refer back to Halloween's close association with the onset of winter and the final harvest.

Precisely how Halloween was observed or understood in Britain depended upon a variety of factors: the strength of oral tradition, the structure of the economy, and the religious culture. There is little evidence that the holiday had achieved the uniformity it would in twentieth-century North America. In rural areas, Halloween might be strongly related to the harvest, to the renewal of leases and farm hire, as well as to the world of the supernatural. In some urban areas it could be quite commercialized. Judging from the poems that were written about Edinburgh's Hallow fair in the eighteenth century, Halloween was a secular night for courtship, gaiety, and "gude ale." It was a time when "Love's Stalks are scattered/The top Grain is wasted/And Mause gang [more go] to Kirk [church] anything but a Maid."[66] It was also a night when too much reveling might tempt a young man to heed the hearty words of the recruiting sergeants who were always on the lookout for "sturdy lads."[67]

The diversity of practices associated with Halloween is reflected in the variety of words by which the holiday was known. In the lengthy testimony submitted to the National Folklore Commission in Ireland, for example, we find that Halloween was often called Hollantide or All Holland, or in Northern Ireland, Halleve, terms that reflected its Christian past. In County Connaught and County Kildare it was also known as Puca Night, a reference to the imps who purportedly befouled the fruit and crops still in the fields and also to the mischief-making mummers who came to the door in "all sorts of fantastic disguises."[68] The centrality of masking was also apparent in the terms used in County Wicklow and County Mayo: Vizor or Vazards Night; Juggy Night or Blackman's Night, a reference to the entertainers who visited neighbors and blackened their faces with burnt cork; Hugata Night, after the boys or *hugaidhes* who went around dressed like tramps; and Bredeogs Night, a reference either to the wicker baskets that mummers may have used to collect gifts or to the wicker masks or visors that they wore. Other terminology was more contemporary, referring to the games or pranks that were traditionally played at Halloween: Snap Apple Night; Colcannon Night, referring to the potato dish in which rings or sixpences were hidden; and Gate Night, an allusion to the practice of unhinging farmers' gates and leaving them at the crossroads.

The diversity of names associated with Halloween did not connote the declining fortunes of the holiday. In Scotland, Ireland, and even in some of the remoter areas of England and Wales, Halloween was robustly observed throughout the nineteenth century and into the twentieth. At the time of substantial Irish and Scottish immigration to North America, Halloween had a strong tradition of guising and pranks, a fundamental aura of supernatural intensity, and a set of games and rituals that often addressed the fortunes of love rather than the prospect of death, or life beyond death. How these practices developed in North America is a subject we address next.

❆ 3 ❆
COMING OVER
Halloween in North America

Halloween did not take firm root in North America until the nineteenth century. The Puritans of New England, like their counterparts in the old country, detested the holiday. Increase Mather, the rector of Harvard, approved of the ban on saints' days and thought any holiday suffixed -mass, whether Hallowmass or even Christmas, to be an unnecessary concession to the Antichrist.[1] His son, Cotton Mather, concurred. In this Zion in the wilderness, in this land of "Uprightness," reveling holidays were out. Even to talk of specters and apparitions tended to smack of witchcraft,[2] and superstitious souls who remembered the magic of Halloween were likely wary of making their feelings felt.

North American almanacs of the late eighteenth and early nineteenth century give no indication that Halloween was recognized as a holiday. New York, Boston, and even San Francisco almanacs highlighted the Gunpowder Plot, the Fifth of November, and made token gestures to All Souls' and All Saints', but 31 October called for no comment. One New England almanac for 1776 simply stated that it "ends the month."

In the light of the transatlantic migrations of the nineteenth century, however, it was likely that Halloween would be celebrated in some form or other in North America. The vast numbers of Irish men and women who crossed the Atlantic, and the persistent outflow of Scots as well, ensured that the festival would serve as a marker of ethnic identity. By 1890, nearly two million Irish men and women lived in the United States. Indeed, the Irish-Americans and their descendants outnumbered all other immigrant groups combined well into the twentieth century. The number of Scottish people who ventured to the United States was significantly smaller, although in the last three decades of the nineteenth century it was the destination of the majority of Scots who left the British Isles. Scottish emigration to Canada had been higher in the century prior to 1870, so the Scottish presence there vied with that of the Irish. In 1881, of the English or Gaelic-speaking peoples of Canada, 33 percent were of Irish and 25 percent of Scottish descent. Thus, at the turn of the century, the Irish were the predominant immigrant minority in the United States; in Canada, the Irish and Scots outnumbered those of English extraction by a ratio of seven to five.

In Canada and the United States, 31 October was never regarded as a sectarian holiday, that is, as one that might have differentiated Catholics from Protestants. The days of Orange-Green confrontations were predictably those cherished by each group: St. Patrick's Day, the anniversary of the patron saint of Ireland, and 12 July, the anniversary of the Battle of the Boyne.[3] Very occasionally, violence spilled onto the streets on Guy Fawkes Day, a day still commemorated by Bostonians and Protestant Canadians. In 1864, for example, trouble flared in Toronto during the Orange Order's celebrations of the holiday. On this occasion, it was rumored that the Orangemen planned to burn effigies of Daniel O'Connell, the Catholic Irish liberator, and also of the Duke of Newcastle, the colonial secretary who had demanded that the Order remove a transparency of William III from the triumphal arch greeting the Prince of Wales in 1860.[4] But Halloween was not an occasion specifically targeted for this kind of sectarian politics.

There were efforts, in fact, to recast Halloween as a day of decorous ethnic celebration. The impetus behind this in Canada came from the well-heeled Caledonian Society. Founded in 1855 by members of the

Scottish-Canadian elite, many of whom were well placed in business and higher education, this society observed Halloween with an annual concert of Highland reels, jigs, ballads, and the poems of Robbie Burns. As a guest speaker remarked at the 1885 Montreal meeting, "we are not divining the future, or burning nuts, or catching the 'snap apple,' but [we are] celebrating Scottishness."[5] He went on to applaud the industry and enterprise of the Scots, and their important contribution to Canadian life. "In the legislature, in the pulpit, in the counting house, on the farm," he proclaimed, "everywhere—Scotchmen are successful." For the Caledonian societies of Canada, then, Halloween became an opportunity to expatiate on the Scottish contribution to nation-building and empire and to honor its more auspicious representatives. These included Lord Strathcona, the governor-general at the turn of the century, who was said to epitomize the "true type of the Highland chief," a man who had used his "great wealth to bind all classes together."[6]

In the interests of elite solidarity and mutual tolerance, the Montreal branch of the Caledonian Society also invited representatives from other ethnic societies to its annual junkets. In 1900 they included the presidents of the St. George and St. Patrick societies, the St. Jean Baptiste Society, and the Irish Protestant Benevolent Society. By 1910, prominent local businessmen from the Montreal Irish community were also in attendance. Yet there is no indication that Halloween was celebrated as a pan-Celtic event; rather, it centered upon "Auld Scotia" and the gritty qualities that brought Scotsmen success along the St. Lawrence.[7]

Few societies were as self-congratulatory as the Caledonian, but many seized the opportunity to use Halloween to rally their supporters and consolidate their membership. This was the case with the Orkney and Shetland Society of Hamilton, which organized a Halloween concert with a "strong Scotch flavour" in 1893. It was also true of the Young Ireland Literary Society of this industrial town, of the Hibernian Knights of Montreal, and the Kingston Sons of Scotland. In New York City, the Irish National League held a Halloween ball at the Lexington

Avenue opera house in 1887, while a branch of the Gaelic Society on West 28th Street held a *seannches*, that is, an evening of poetry and music, the same year.[8] North of the border, Orangemen also celebrated Halloween with concerts and balls. In Kingston, Ontario, the 'Prentice Boys and Orange Young Britons regularly held an assembly and ball at the Victoria Music Hall.[9] The Hamilton lodge did so in 1872, but the following year, they switched the date to 5 November, the anniversary of the Gunpowder Plot.[10] The reasons for this are unclear, but it might have been a response to the growing sectarian violence within the Irish population that was filling the streets of Ontario's major cities.[11]

Philadelphia, which had a sizable Irish population in the nineteenth century, was also home to a variety of Halloween celebrations. In the 1860s, the curious could venture to Mrs. Drew's New Arch Street Theatre to hear storyteller Barney Williams entertain them with "those legendary dreams of Old Ireland." Alternatively, they could go to the quadrille party held at Mr. Shaw's academy at Washington Hall,[12] or even to the local firemen's bash.[13] And there was always the tavern for those who wanted a few drams or the pleasure of gawking at revelers in "fancy costume." In Philadelphia, in particular, where there was a rich tradition of masquerading in the streets on festive occasions, particularly at the New Year, Halloween must have been a colorful affair. By the turn of the century, it was said that the streets were filled with "thousands of persons intent on enjoyment that would hardly have been countenanced by the worthy Quaker founders of the city."[14]

Because of the peculiarities of newspaper reporting, we know less about the family side of Halloween in the nineteenth century than we do about its more public face at balls and concerts. But it is clear that Halloween was being adapted to the urban milieu of North America, in which a conspicuous minority of Irish immigrants congregated.[15] Judging from the accounts in the *New York Herald*, "fireside games" abounded, with Scottish and Irish immigrants humorously reenacting the contests and fortune-telling of their forebears and dressing up for the occasion. "The forests and dells of the United States are too cold and tramp-infested to be thickly populated with fairies and witches," remarked the *Herald* with amusement in 1878, "but American ingenuity has devised an acceptable substitute, so if any one failed to see dancing fairies and witches innumerable last evening, it was because he did not make a tour of the parlours of his acquaintances."[16]

Predictably, Halloween was being celebrated in more commercial venues and in more commercial ways. Advertisements in the *British Whig Weekly* reveal that Halloween masks could be bought in local Kingston, Ontario stores as early as 1874. Within fifteen years it was quite casually remarked that "the run on masks" was "abnormal."[17] Grocers and wholesale merchants also cashed in on the celebration. A wide variety of nuts was advertised for the holiday: pecans, almonds, walnuts, chestnuts, filberts, and Brazil nuts. By the end of the nineteenth century, this festive fare had expanded considerably. Figs, raisins, Florida oranges, and Malaga grapes were eagerly sought, in addition to the seasonal apple. And the taste for candy of contemporary Halloween was already being cultivated. One advertisement for 1897 reads: "Special for Hallowe'en at Carson's—Chocolates 10c and 15c lb; creams 10c and 15c lb; gumdrops 10c and 15c lb; all taffies 15c per lb. Oysters served in every style. Ice cream on order."[18]

Perhaps the best indication that the customs of Halloween were changing centered on the decline of its divinatory rites and superstitions. "The glory of this once popular festival," remarked the *New York Times*, in 1876, "has departed."[19]

> Its triumphs and rough jollities, festivals and strange rites
> are a matter of history, and live only in the immortal verse
> of Burns and traditional lore. The timid Amaryllis of these
> more prosaic times does not trust her matrimonial fate to
> the doubtful chance of picking out, blindfolded, the basin
> of dirty or clean water, or of depending for a "weel taur'd"
> man on the likelihood of "pooling" [pulling] at the stroke

of midnight a straight-rooted "kail runt." There are still kept up in the western and rural parts of southern Scotland and Ireland some of the rough old games so peculiar to this festival, but over the world, wherever Scotchmen, Englishmen or Irishmen are domiciled, the trail of civilization is over them all. Evening parties, with a ring hid mysteriously away in some elegant work of the pastry cook's genius, have taken the place of the great "black pot" full of mashed potatoes and milk. The rough reel and jig have been replaced by the seductive waltz or pleasant quadrille, and the hilarious "hoohs" and clatter of hob nailed boots . . . mingling in inharmonious numbers with the squeaking of a villainous old fiddle have been succeeded by the rustling of silks . . . and the strains of the high-toned centennial prize piano forte. Like the curious marriage and funeral customs of old . . . the old halloween revelries are gone. Even in New York, among the Scottish inhabitants, they live in memory only as traditions.

We should allow for journalistic license here, and recognize that Halloween has been framed within the familiar narrative of converting every immigrant into a putative middle-class citizen. It is doubtful that the "old halloween revelries" had entirely disappeared, or that the pianoforte had replaced the tin whistle, fiddle, and uilleann pipes in the tenements of New York or in the wooden shacks of Canadian towns along Lake Ontario and the St. Lawrence. But it does seem that the divinatory practices of Halloween so prevalent in rural Scotland and Ireland were losing their appeal. The *Montreal Gazette* attributed this to the civilizing influence of North American cities, noting the decline of these "more frivolous and petty celebrations" in favor of more "literary or more rational enjoyments."[20] Yet it is likely that their decline was also related to the different demographic profiles of urban life and to the changing patterns of courtship that high mobility into the city brought with it. Young men and women did not leave home any earlier than in previous centuries; in fact, overall, teenagers likely left home rather later and in smaller numbers. But they increasingly entered unsupervised environments, often outside the conventional channels of domestic service and apprenticeship and with greater access to wage-labor markets. Consequently, they had greater opportunities to flaunt their sexuality and to find their own partners.[21] Halloween in the big city was fun, but it was no longer part of a community-regulated courtship cycle, as it had been in the villages of Scotland and Ireland. As early as 1831, an Upper Canadian newspaper was poking fun at the love spells that marked Halloween, reminding readers that marriage was a lottery anyway, with or without "the popping of a parched acorn."[22] Halloween continued to be of special significance to "love-lorn swains and maidens," so the *New York Herald* remarked in 1872, but its divinations were games that ended in mock-marriages rather than real ones.[23]

The shape and spirit of middle-class Halloween can be imagined from three prints in the *Canadian Illustrated News* of the 1870s and 1880s. The first, in 1872, depicts a family celebrating Halloween with relatives and friends. On the left, a fashionably dressed woman, probably the wife of the household, is either roasting chestnuts or placing two nuts together to see how they will react, closely watched by her daughters and her husband. In the background, two other ladies are entertaining guests by divining her future, one with cards, the other with egg white. In the foreground, a party-groomed boy is offering a girl a chestnut, while behind group of boys and girls are dunking for apples. The engraving conveys an atmosphere of relaxed amusement, acting out time-honored customs in the respectable space of a middle-class parlor.

The two other prints offer variations to this domestic theme. In one, a young women ponders her reflection in the mirror, hoping to catch a glimpse of her future husband, not the "aged cavalier" who gapes back at her. In the other, there are sketches of games similar to those of 1872— roasting nuts, dunking for apples—although this time time blind-man's

Halloween in the middle-class parlor, from *Canadian Illustrated News*, 1872.

bluff has been added to the repertoire. Yet the predominantly adult partygoers are more animated. Chairs are toppled, men and women clamber on tables, and a fiddler rolls out a reel for the dancers. In the center, another fashion-conscious young woman hazards her future in the mirror while eating an apple. Above her, the apple-dunking barrel spills out its contents, providing an oblique reference to the pranks of the evening.

None of these prints provides any clue to the outdoor activities of Halloween. In view of the conventions of respectability within middle-class households, this is predictable. It would have been improper for middle-class youngsters, particularly women, to gad about the streets in fantastical guises. This was more likely to occur among the teenagers of the working class, especially males, whose revels and everyday interactions habitually spilled out beyond their cramped living quarters. "The old time custom of keeping up Hallowe'en was not forgotten last night by the youngsters of the city," reported the Kingston, Ontario,

Daily News in 1866. "They had their maskings and their merry-makings, and perambulated the streets after dark in a way which no doubt was mightily amusing to themselves. There was a great sacrifice of pumpkins from which to make transparent heads and face, lighted up by the unfailing two inches of tallow candle."[24]

The making of jack-o'-lanterns was an adaptation of the old custom of commemorating souls in purgatory with candles cradled in turnips. As befitted the custom, guisers visited private houses to solicit gifts, although these now included "cakes, apples, nuts, and money,"[25] normally in return for a rhyme or song for their hosts. This sort of merry-making or mummery was also found on the street, where local bands sometimes volunteered their services. In 1893, the Orange Young Britons fife-and-drum band paraded through the streets of Kingston on Halloween, decked out in silk ties and burned-cork faces. According to the newspapers, the band "afforded much amusement for the boys" who congregated in "their 'get-ups,' singing, laughing and dancing."[26]

Revelers were usually given a "special license" to be merry on Halloween, and the public normally respected the tradition. It was expected that passers-by would donate nickels, dimes, or quarters to the masqueraders, and local stores were frequently besieged for treats.[27] Neighborly pranks were also very much a part of the festive raillery. It was customary to root up vegetables from backyard gardens, disfigure jack-o'-lanterns on front steps or porches, unhinge gates and shutters, tip over outhouses, pull down signs and fences, and even tear up the wooden boarded sidewalks. In rural areas, farm implements and cart wheels might even be placed on roofs. At Hartington, a small township just north of Kingston, where the "boys were out in full force" on Halloween in 1892, inhabitants discovered a freight car across the roadway the following morning "loaded with all sorts of truck."[28] In the cities, delivery vans were sometimes moved to other streets and pranksters tried to unhook the poles from streetcars and temporarily immobilize them. In Kingston, revelers greased the tracks on steep inclines, forcing the transit authorities to scatter sand on them before the trolley cars could proceed. In Halifax, Nova Scotia, in 1900, a dummy was placed on the car tracks at Gottingen Street, forcing an unsuspecting driver to grind to a sharp stop.[29]

The more serious pranks were carried out by older boys late at night. They prompted an ongoing debate about how much vandalism would be tolerated on this raucous night. The fledgling police forces of nineteenth-century cities spent a good deal of their time trying to clear the streets of rowdy and unsavory elements, especially drunks and prostitutes; and their vigilance was closely monitored by temperance and philanthropic societies that wanted to make urban spaces more decorous, orderly, and accessible to respectable citizens. Was Halloween to be the exception that proved the rule?

Until the end of the nineteenth century, at least, the police gave revelers a pretty wide berth. In 1898, it was reported that the Halifax police gave several street gangs "a bad scare" but declined to arrest anyone.[30] Youthful pranks were tolerated, provided they did not inflict too much damage to property or endanger life. Merrymakers were reprimanded for derailing streetcars because of the potential injury it could inflict upon passengers. Bonfires were extinguished as potential fire hazards.[31] Yet when Kingston revelers ripped up awnings and tore down fences in 1872, a newspaper simply remarked that this was "serious play . . . lads will be lads."[32] The same tolerance could be found in the following lines from Toronto:

> Now the urchin hath his fun,
> The reign of terror's now begun,
> For Hallowe'en is here.[33]

Not everybody was so light-hearted about the damage that was caused on Halloween, some of which took days, even weeks, to repair. Predictably, there were a few instances where Halloween pranks found their way into the police courts. In 1870, three Kingston youths were fined $3 each for throwing stones at the window of Mary Shippey and striking her when she attempted to remonstrate with them.[34] Two years earlier, a gang of street urchins plagued an unpopular neighbor in the run-up to Halloween by persistently knocking his door, bespattering his windows with mud, and even pitching dead cats into the passage beside his house. These nocturnal pranks culminated in a "perfect carnival of juvenile horrors" on Halloween itself, provoking the householder, one William Farr, to attack one of the gang. When called upon to defend his actions in police court, Farr claimed the boys had so "distracted his mind" that he impulsively took "summary justice upon the juvenile tyrants" by clubbing one of them over the head. The magistrate was not impressed with this defense, and fined Farr $2 plus costs. In the interests of public order, he "administered a rebuke to the boys for being on the streets at night."[35] It was an odd rebuke for prankish Halloween, and one that could hardly have been taken seriously.

By the turn of the nineteenth century, the tolerance for rowdiness and vandalism on Halloween was wearing thin in some quarters. In Chatham, Ontario, several boys were forced to compensate a householder for transferring his outhouse to rougher ground. In Hamilton, two lads and a girl were taken to court for pulling down a smokestack and placing a bobsleigh on the roof. One of the boys thought this quite unfair, claiming he had been told he "would not be touched as it was Halloween."[36] In Kingston, the Halloween spree of 1902 led to an estimated $1500 worth of damage to fences and sidewalks and an assault upon a second-hand clothes dealer who had tried to protect his wagon from revelers. As a result, downtown merchants demanded police protection from this vandalism. From 1903 until 1914, the authorities obliged by swearing in special constables on Halloween, a policy that seems to have curbed "old-time rowdyism."[37] In 1917, a Kingston newspaper remarked that "the rough element among the boys" was less evident on Halloween.[38]

Like their Canadian counterparts, urban dwellers in the United States were increasingly confronted with the problem of youthful disorder on

Halloween, and their response was correspondingly mixed. In 1905, the *Chicago Daily Journal* printed a cartoon that depicted barrels on steeples; clothes on telegraph wires; wagons on barns; gates, umbrellas, and milk cans on rooftops; and beer advertisements defacing church porches. The cartoon came with the caption, "Halloween Boisterous? Oh! Please don't mention it. You were a youngster once on a time yourself."[39] Two years later, the *New York Herald* produced another cartoon that portrayed Halloween in an amusing light. It showed street kids tripping up gentlemen, frightening old ladies with ghoulish pumpkins, removing store signs, boisterously dunking apples, and splattering one another with flour.

Not all people shared the *Herald*'s humor, however. One turn-of-the-century newspaper thought that Halloween tricks "committed under the shade of darkness" were "cowardly" and advised readers to "load their muskets or cannon with rock, salt or bird shot and when the trespasses invade your premises at unseemly hours . . . pepper them good or proper."[40] Few public reactions were as militant as this, but many were certainly alarmed by the rough revelry and growing vandalism that accompanied Halloween. "It is to be regretted that the spirit of rowdyism has in a measure superseded the kindly old customs," William Walsh observed in 1897.

> In towns and villages gangs of hoodlums throng the streets, ringing the doorbells and wrenching the handles from their sockets and taking gates off their hinges. In Washington boys carry flour in a bag. Care is taken to have the web of the bag so that a slight blow will release a generous supply of white powder. . . . These the boys use upon one another as well as upon non-belligerent passers-by.[41]

In New York City, kids sometimes substituted black stockings filled with ashes for flour-bags. In the novel *A Tree Grows in Brooklyn*, one of the characters blackened his face with soot on Halloween, and with "cap

Halloween pranks, New York City, from the *New York Herald*, 1907.

backwards" and "coat inside out," roamed the streets with his gang, "swinging his homely blackjack and crying out raucously from time to time."[42] The same rite was exercised in Chicago, where young men and boys routinely made "soot bag attacks" on passers-by, forcing young women to seek refuge in drug stores and dwellings.[43] Similar antics were practiced in Philadelphia, where "companies of youths" marched "in the garbs of all nations armed with bean shooters, inflated bags, stuffed stockings, horns and other equipment for the fun-making."[44]

These street encounters were deplored by law-abiding citizens, who felt that harassing young women, in particular, was mean-spirited and unmanly. Consequently, there were attempts to curb the practice through police and court action. Special details of police were ordered to contain the festive exuberance of merrymakers on Halloween, and local courts routinely dealt with youthful offenders after a night of fun and hilarity. In 1907, some 200 people found themselves before the Chicago courts after a night's raucous merrymaking.[45] Yet overstretched police forces were not always able to contain the night's activity. In 1904, for example, the *New York Herald* reported a spree of flour-bag bashing upon unwary pedestrians on East 13th Street. Those inside their houses had the discomfort of seeing their iron gates unhinged and placed elsewhere. One manager of a leather goods company was angry enough about these antics to remonstrate with the revelers and have one twelve-year-old arrested by the police. He must have regretted his response. For two hours, an angry mob of 300 boys besieged the police station where he was giving his testimony, and the crowd was dispersed only when reinforcements arrived from another precinct.[46] As the *Montreal Gazette* observed in 1910, "the new Hallowe'en of American cities" was developing a reputation for being "quite unhallowed."[47]

If urban youths were revitalizing Halloween as a night of hilarious pranks and disorder, the holiday was also being coopted by university students in the form of rags or rushes. In Toronto, and to a lesser extent at Queen's (Kingston) and McGill (Montreal), university students took to the streets on Halloween, chanting in packs, moving signs, and uprooting railings, and sometimes even immobilizing street cars. Some U.S. colleges and universities celebrated Halloween as raucously. Northwestern students, for example, went on painting sprees of campus property and downtown stores. In 1907, thirty-one of them were arrested for hosing down divinity students in their dormitory.[48] Chicago students turned Halloween into a territorial battle for class flags, scaling the 135-foot smokestack of the heating plant to fly their own colors and assert their supremacy. Medical students at Ann Arbor even spirited away cadavers from the anatomy laboratory. In 1900 they propped up the corpse of a headless woman against the folding doors of University Hall.[49]

Most U.S. students appear to have celebrated Halloween in a more orderly fashion. In Michigan, Olivet College held a Halloween barbecue at which the sophomores dressed up in ghostly costumes and danced, like Shakespeare's witches in *Macbeth*, around a "boiling cauldron."[50] At the Detroit College of Medicine, students marched through the streets in a "'shirt-tail' parade," many of them "rigged up grotesquely."[51] At Wellesley and Barnard College, female students appropriated the occasion to foreground their marginal status as voters and citizens. In 1912, they conducted a mock debate between the five presidential

candidates in the upcoming election and voted on which they found
the most eligible for the White House. The students of New York
University, in contrast, observed Halloween as a hazing rite for
freshmen. These novices were forced to join a parade in their
nightgowns to the houses of the president, the dean, and other members
of the faculty. They were then "exhibited" before the assembled student
body and obliged to disclose their name, age, and politics, sing the
school song, and give the school yell. Finally, they were ducked or
"baptized" in the Hall of Fame fountain.[52]

The president of NYU thought this hazing rite a pretty harmless
affair, more conducive to the *esprit de corps* of the college than to
Halloween rowdyism. His Canadian counterparts must have viewed
the rituals of their students more ambivalently. In the 1870s and early
1880s, students celebrated Halloween by blocking up lecture halls,
catcalling faculty, and generally enjoying themselves with seasonal
hilarity. From the mid-1880s onward, however, beginning in Toronto,
students marched to the local theaters or opera house and made a
nuisance of themselves from the upper gallery or the boxes, catcalling,
hooting, and generally making their presence felt. From the pit they
appeared as "a blur of black and white," one newspaper reported, a
"many-headed monster [which] surged and heaved and raised unceasing
bedlam, never desisting from pawing the floor and hammering with
bludgeons."[53]

Much of the bustle was good-natured enough. Students normally
congregated under their collegial colors, which they draped over the
balcony. Sometimes they added humorous signs or artifacts. The School
of Science embellished their box in 1902 with boards reading "Rogues
Gallery" and "Wild Animals I have Known." Trinity students dangled a
skeleton over their portion of the rail on one occasion, and those in
Practical Science once dangled a live chicken. In keeping with the season,
actresses were greeted with mixed messages. One leading lady was
presented with a huge floral skull and crossbones. In Montreal, "Old
McGill" unloaded a "small sized flower shop" on the lady performers,

exaggerating to a point of parody the bouquet of flowers conventionally offered to female artists.[54] All this was a prelude to the real intent of the evening, which was to turn the performance into an uproarious vaudeville, to appropriate it for the students. Villains and cads were hissed; lovers applauded. Pathetic scenes were greeted with catcalls or moans. And if the disruption to the artists was formidable enough, the city burghers in the stalls had their pates peppered with peas, while young women were pestered with paper darts or falling bunting.

The fashionably dressed audiences were not unduly bothered by the uproarious humor of the students. Some of them likely recognized their own sons and brothers in the gallery, or those of their professional neighbors. This was, after all, a collegial coming-out party, a ritual celebrating student exuberance at the expense of those who had already established themselves in professional or business life. Students were part of the show and were allowed to express their own marginality as society's next, but as yet unestablished, leaders in good-humored banter and mockery.

Tempers did flare, however, when theater managers attempted to restrict the number of students in the galleries. Scuffles were reported between the Queen's students and the police when they were refused admittance to the Grand Opera House in 1919. The following year, students used a battering ram to try to break in, a precedent that cost them a stiff fine of $26 for disorderly conduct.[55]

The most dramatic confrontations with authority took place on the marches to the theaters, or during the revels afterward. Students marched aggressively to the theaters waving their colors and canes and hooting at passers-by. In what was a symbolic invasion of the town by the gown, trouble inevitably ensued as police sought to control the antics and prevent damage to gas lanterns and windows. These antics resumed after the performances. In Toronto, students normally proceeded uptown to serenade the young women who lived in the residences of various elite girls' schools. Some then dispersed to various parties, while others went on to visit faculty or prominent citizens. On the way, the usual Halloween vandalism was inflicted upon signs, windows, gas lamps, and fences. When the damage to property was wanton, the police usually moved in.

The police found themselves in a somewhat difficult position in dealing with students, many of whom were well connected and made this patently clear to the constables on duty. As the Kingston *Daily Standard* noted, students often felt they owned the city and were "privileged persons who are superior to the law."[56] In these circumstances, the police must have wondered whether arrests were worth the effort, given the small fines that were often inflicted upon students by

The police curbing student revels in Toronto, from the *Toronto Evening News*, 1908.

genial magistrates. They chafed at the way in which students were able to avoid the law when vandalism or rowdiness occurred on university property, on the grounds that the proper disciplinary authority on these occasions were the colleges themselves. Very occasionally, the police overreacted in their dealings with students. In 1902, five mounted policemen clubbed medical students leaving a faculty reception in Toronto, apparently without provocation.[57] But usually the police dealt with the students in an even-handed manner, especially given the taunts and provocations they had to endure from people whom they regarded as trouble-making snobs on their way up in the world.

The years 1884–1920 were those when college students appropriated Halloween for their own purposes. They used Halloween's rites of inversion and revelry to haze freshmen, as at NYU, or to frame the initiation rituals of freshettes, as at Queen's University in Kingston.[58] In the case of Toronto, Halloween revels were used to consolidate collegial identities after hazing. Marches or "rushes" to the theaters were occasions when students marked their presence in town life, razzed their superiors, and thumbed their noses at authority generally. It was a moment of inversion for a privileged population moving from adolescence to young adulthood and perhaps anxious about their future place or chances of success in society. In fact, there is no evidence that college students felt any special bond of sympathy with lower-class revelers in defying authority and ragging unpopular professors. Indeed, when students did move beyond the familiar rites of campus inversion, they sometimes ran into trouble. In 1903, for example, eighty McGill students ventured into Longueuil on Halloween for some prankish fun but were driven into the St. Lawrence River by the locals. Fifty of them were reportedly injured.[59]

By the 1920s, student rags on Halloween were disappearing. University administrations discouraged downtown rushes in the light of increasing civic displeasure. Yet the decline of Halloween student revels was also related to changes in the school calendar. As long as students returned to the university in October, the appropriation of Halloween as a liminal moment in the school year made sense. When students began to return to campus earlier in the year, as they did in the 1920s, Halloween's significance as a student *rite de passage* declined.

The raucous observance of Halloween by students at the turn of the century nonetheless points to a more general phenomenon: the emergence of the holiday as a fixture in the North American calendar. In the mid-nineteenth century, Halloween had been regarded as a preeminently Irish or Scottish festival, as one observed by immigrants or first-generation Americans of Irish or Scottish descent.[60] This notion persisted into the 1890s, when journalists still pondered whether the holiday would become anything more than an ethnic-identified festival. Yet as early as 1875, one newspaper noted that many Americans besides "our Irish adopted citizens" were celebrating Halloween.[61] The adoption of Halloween by students was one measure that it was becoming more generally observed; so, too, was its adoption by town socialites. In Toronto, Halloween opened the winter's season of private dinner parties and public entertainments.[62] From 1886 onward, Manhattan debutantes held an annual Halloween ball at Tuxedo Park. Charity balls and parties soon followed. In 1895, for example, the Red Cross held a Halloween party at the Brooklyn Art Gallery, at which 350 guests wore Highland costume and danced the Gay Gordons. By the first decade of the twentieth century, country clubs in Lenox, Massachusetts, Lexington, Kentucky, and Hot Springs, Virginia, routinely held Halloween parties and roasts. By 1910, Halloween was fully integrated into the social calendar of the Washington elite.

Elite sponsorship undoubtedly helped consolidate Halloween's place in both the Canadian and U.S. calendar. Yet its popularity was also growing among the population at large. Detroit newspapers made no mention of Halloween in the 1870s, but by 1904, cartoons portrayed Germans playing Halloween pranks. Indeed, because the rituals of Halloween were not that different from those of Martinmass (11 November), German and Dutch immigrants had little difficulty in taking to the holiday, with societies such as the German American

Democratic candidate William Jennings Bryan, divining his fate on
Halloween before the 1900 presidential election, from the *Chicago Daily
Tribune*, 1900.

Benevolent Association holding Halloween dinners and dances.[63] African-Americans were celebrating Halloween, as well. In 1903 in Chicago, their revels resulted in an unfortunate stabbing of a policeman and a near lynching of the blacks involved. In fact, so general was the observance of the holiday that the town of Albany, New York, organized a two-day Halloween carnival in 1905 that was attended by an estimated 50,000 visitors from across the state.[64] As a nonethnic holiday, Halloween had clearly arrived. It was a familiar enough festival to merit a cartoon that depicted the Democratic candidate William Jennings Bryan attempting to divine his fate in the 1900 presidential election. A few years later, another cartoon depicted a Chicago beef baron frightened by a pumpkin-faced attorney bent on prosecuting the packer under antitrust law.[65]

If Halloween was clearly broadening its social constituency in towns of the East and Midwest, it was also moving westward. In 1908, Halloween "roysterers" at Belton, Texas, burned freight cars, houses, and 1000 bales of cotton in a night of fire that cost as much as $250,000.[66] Two years later, the *San Francisco Chronicle* reported a Halloween entertainment and dance sponsored by a Ladies Aid Society in West Oakland, and the *Los Angeles Times* featured a cartoon entitled "The Halloween Game," in which four lawyers vied for the job of district attorney in Los Angeles county. At the same time, large stores such as Jevne's of Broadway and Spring Street claimed that it was "incomparably the best place to supply all the last-minute needs and finishing touches for the Hallowe'en festivities."[67] The holiday had arrived on the West Coast.

How can we explain Halloween's promotion to national status? Part of the answer lies in the fact Halloween happened to coincide roughly with the resumption of parliamentary or congressional business in state, provincial, and federal capitals; with U.S. federal elections; and with the beginning of the social season. As a holiday observed by leading immigrant groups, it was no doubt diplomatic to incorporate it into the political and social calendar. Because it was pan-Celtic and not identified with any one interest, this could be achieved without a loss of political goodwill.

Yet Halloween also drew its appeal from the fact that it continued to be a night of social inversion and youthful exuberance in an era when other holidays became increasingly home-centered, respectable, and institutionalized. In the early nineteenth century this was not the case at all. There were a number of holidays when high-spirited people could celebrate on the streets. Although the Fifth of November did not have the same vitality or political resonance that it had in the precolonial era, it could still generate a lot of mischievous fun in East Coast towns such as Portsmouth, New Hampshire, as well as in Orange-dominated towns such as Toronto.[68] In Newfoundland, which was settled by Irish Catholics and by English Protestants from the Atlantic ports, Halloween and Bonfire Night coexisted in a raucous season that ran from late October to mid-November. Whereas Halloween was until quite recently celebrated with torch-burning parades, pranks, and forms of "mummery," the Fifth of November was devoted to building huge bonfires, at least in the predominantly Protestant communities. From early October, adolescent boys would collect and sometimes steal wood, blubber barrels, and tires for bonfires that were fifteen feet high and twenty to thirty feet in diameter. Several inhabitants from Barr'd Islands and Joe Batt's Arm remembered one that consisted of seventy-five barrels and twenty tires, not to mention the thousands of boughs that were cut from the local woods.[69] Once these huge fires had died away, older boys might resort to playing pranks, such as setting old boats alight. Recalling his adventures in the late 1950s, one resident of Flower's Cove remarked: "We would then hide in the grass or behind something, and wait for the owner to turn up. After he arrived he would go in a rage and chase after us. If anyone was caught he was given a beating."[70]

Even without Bonfire Night, Halloween faced wintry competitors from other holidays in nineteenth-century North America. In New England, there were "Negro Election" days during which blacks celebrated their new "Governor" with dancing, fiddling, and drinking.[71]

In Philadelphia and rural Pennsylvania, revelrous Santas called Belsnickles (a variant of the German phrase *Pelz-nickle*, or St. Nicholas in fur) roamed the streets at Christmastide, dressed in cast-off clothing with monstrous or blackened faces. The same tradition existed in the German-based community of Lunenburg in Nova Scotia.[72] Like Halloween tricksters and Christmas mummers, these revelers demanded treats from shopkeepers and citizens and were not above vandalizing property or seizing the streets from rival gangs. In Pottstown, Pennsylvania, in 1826, Belsnickles demolished a back street house belonging to a poor woman and blockaded the main road with barrels, grocery boxes, harrows, and plows.[73]

In New York, too, Christmastide was a time of open-house boozing and revelry, especially on New Year's Eve, when pranksters perambulated the streets with their discordant music. In 1828, the celebrations turned into an ugly riot that the local watch proved powerless to control, prompting calls for a more professional police force to handle the unruly merriment that the season brought with it. Even so, as late as 1851 the New York *Tribune* complained of the "Saturnalia of discord, by Callithumpian and Cowbellian bands, by musketry and fire-crackers, by bacchanal songs and noisy revels, which for two hours after midnight made sleep not a thing to be dreamed of."[74]

During the second half of the nineteenth century, these rougher Yuletide customs were finally brought under firmer civic control. Over time, they became increasingly marginal to the celebration of the Christmas season, which had traditionally lasted twelve nights. This was because Christmas was increasingly being cast in a middle-class idiom. From 1850 onward, it became a more decorous, family-centered affair, featuring Santa Claus, Christmas trees, home-visiting, church-going, and new patterns of consumption that both incorporated and displaced the holiday's discordant elements. One can track this transformation in the changing image of Santa himself, who began the nineteenth century as a mischievous, lecherous street peddler and ended it as the convivial, paunchy, hearty gift-giver, the amiable grandfather figure whom we all know. One can also trace it in the displacement of Christmas mummery and tomfoolery into the Santa Claus parades of the early twentieth century, sponsored in most cities by large department stores such as Gimbel's in Philadelphia (1920), Hudson's in Detroit (1923), and Macy's in New York (1924).[75] In the transformation of Christmas into a rite of consumption, charity, and decorous conviviality, Philadelphia's belsnickling was also brought under civic supervision and turned into a Mummer's Parade organized by local clubs. As Susan Davis has noted, this meant that "the noisy strains of youth culture receded from the festival's core."[76]

While Yuletide was being recast in a middle-class idiom, Orange lodges and Hibernian societies celebrated their holidays more decorously, or at least actively discouraged any rowdyism that might tarnish their new-won social and political reputation. The triumph of respectability was predictably a protracted affair, whose temporalities could differ from town to town. In Toronto, Irish ethnic festivals were more or less tamed by the 1880s. In Worcester, Massachusetts, Irish temperance societies battled with revelers over the celebration of St. Patrick's Day well into the 1890s. The same was true of the Fourth of July celebrations, which were often conducted in an uproarious fashion, with fireworks, fireballs, and "a pandemonium of drums, bells, and every variety of noise."[77] Irish newspapers would insist that the Fourth of July was one of the few occasions when "all restraint is thrown off and noise and confusion reign supreme."[78] But from the 1880s onward, citizens were advised to set up committees to make the celebrations more focused and orderly, and to coordinate local societies for the annual street procession.[79] Within twenty years, picnics, parades, sports, and games were prevailing over bonfires, firecrackers, and drunken vandalism in the celebration of America's independence.

There were inevitably some exceptions to this civilizing process. In New York and other East Coast cities, the American celebration of Thanksgiving, which was first celebrated on a national scale in 1863 thanks to the efforts of matriarchs like Mrs. Sarah Hale, remained a buoyant street festival for "ragamuffins" as much as a sedate, family-centered dinner. George William Douglas noted that "children in the different neighborhoods dressed themselves in clothes of their elders, covered their faces with masks and paraded the streets blowing tin horns."[80] Thus attired, they went from house to house asking for fruit and vegetables to celebrate the day. As late as 1928 it was remarked that the New York streets were "full of 'Ragamuffins'—kids dressed in ridiculous Hallowe'en costumes, begging for pennies."[81]

In the 1890s, Los Angeles developed a raucous spring fiesta that for a decade or so featured mock mayors and elements of social inversion. In New Orleans, Mardi Gras blossomed into a baroque festival that encompassed elite Southerners, marginal blacks and mulattoes, and many thousands of spectators who reveled the night away. This festival of disreputable pleasure, with its street parades and masked balls, some of which took place in high-class brothels, grew out of the complex confluence of cultures and political takeovers of the New World world. Outside the mainstream of American conviviality, it was celebrated only in New Orleans and the neighboring city of Mobile.[82]

By 1900, there were few festivals in North America that had not sifted out their revelrous antics or contained them within institutionalized parades. Halloween was something of an exception. As a Celtic festival never clearly identified with one ethnic minority, it became relatively easy to detach it from its ethnic moorings and revel in its mischief-making potential. Indeed, Halloween appears to have appropriated some of the rituals associated with its rivals; or at the very least, reinvigorated older traditions of masquerading by contact with them. Masking and cross-dressing become more pronounced. And the callithumpian custom of flour-bashing, very visible in the New York riot of 1828 and also observed at Mardi Gras, received a resounding revival. "All the 'vagrom' boys were out in all sort of cheap harlequin and clown disguises, with bags of flour, whitening each other," remarked the New Orleans *Daily Crescent* in 1859 of its Mardi Gras celebrations.[83] It was a description that could have been made of Halloween in New York City or Chicago some forty years later.

In 1857, the *North American Review* mourned the fact that there was "no American festival, absolutely consecrated and universally ack-nowledged," that "hallows the calendar to the imagination of our people." In the author's view, the only potential holiday that had any claim to be national, the Fourth of July, was more of a "noisy carnival" than a "gen-uine patriotic jubilee."[84] Fifty years later, the Fourth of July had become the centerpiece of the American commemorative canon, and a holiday more decorously observed; but quite against the grain of the author's reasoning, there was one holiday that had achieved national, even North American, status without federal sanction, and that was Halloween.

Beginning as an immigrant Celtic festival, Halloween attracted a growing audience across Canada and the United States, to a point that by the first decade of the twentieth century, it was celebrated coast to coast by a wide variety of groups: native and immigrant, rich and poor, black and white, Protestant and Catholic. Halloween had become part of the patrician social season; it was important to the *rites de passage* of college students. As an apple-bobbing night that symbolically inaugurated the wintry season, it was merrily celebrated in North American parlors. And as a night of transgression, that "night of nights for every species of witchcraft and devilry,"[85] it spilled out onto the street, giving even the street urchin his moment of mischief.

Halloween in North America underwent many of the changes that we have already detected in Britain. It became a more secular festival whose supernatural divinations were turned into games such as apple-dunking and nut-cracking. In fact, America's Halloween was arguably celebrated in a more consumerist fashion than its British counterpart by 1900. It had emerged as a commercial red-letter day, with a variety of greeting cards, games, and novelties offered for sale.[86] The holiday's association with All Saints' and All Souls' had also virtually disappeared. Even in a place like New Orleans, where it was customary for people to decorate graves on All Souls' Day, there was a sharp contrast between the revelrous practices of Halloween and the reverential practices that followed, one that emulated the way in which the festive license of Mardi Gras gave way to the solemn duties of Lent.[87]

In the transatlantic crossing there were also changes in Halloween's relationship to the community. When Halloween was celebrated in early nineteenth-century Ireland and Scotland, it was still a community-centered festival that had important ramifications for the agricultural cycle, the courtship of eligible couples, good neighborliness, and the informal exercise of local justice. Transplanted to North America, where Irish and Scottish immigrants often found themselves in more diverse communities engaged in different kinds of work, these aspects of the holiday necessarily waned. Even so, when Halloween first came to America, it continued to be a family-centered festival as well as an evening of nightly revels. The links between these two dimensions of the holiday likely became more attenuated over time, but they continued to be gendered, the familial domain being very much identified with feminine space, and the bonfires, masking, and mischief with the masculine, most notably with male bonding. As Walter Pritchard Eaton noted, when reminiscing of his mid-nineteenth-century childhood, "apple bobbing and trips down the cellar with a lighted candle and a mirror to see your future spouse were all very well for girls and 'dress up' parties. But they weren't the essence of Halloween," at least for boys. That essence was "robbery, destruction, arson."[88]

Over the course of the nineteenth century, the festive spaces of Halloween continued to be gendered in this way. The *Chicago Record* saw Halloween in these terms in 1894, ascribing the courtship games and marriage divinations to the young women and the street pranks to the males.[89] But, increasingly, Halloween also became a peer-group holiday, celebrated in different ways by different generations. It was not without its familial dimension, to be sure, but this was no longer as central as it had been. By the early twentieth century, church groups, high schools, and rotary clubs were taking over some of the domestic rituals of Halloween, sponsoring parties and dances in which many of the games previously reserved for the home were played. And whereas private individuals had relied upon oral tradition for much of their indoor celebrations of the holiday, they increasingly looked to books for tips on how to run a successful Halloween party, whether for children, young adults, or even for young marrieds. One Ohio production recommended that married party-goers identify each other from baby photos and from short anonymous statements of "why I am a model wife/husband." In another game, one clearly related to the Halloweeen convention of fortune telling, the guide also suggested that young women count off rice kernels to the following rhyme:

> Rich girl, poor girl, suffragette
> Waitress, milliner, farmerette
> School ma'am, actress, stenographer
> Musician, train'd nurse, dressmaker;
> Book-keeper, house-maid, author, clerk,
> Telephone girl, and a lazy smirk.[90]

Because harvest thanksgivings were scheduled on different days in Canada and the United States, the importance of Halloween as a familial harvest supper diminished, even though some of the harvest symbolism surrounding Halloween survived: nuts, apples, and pumpkins, for example. No doubt, families played an important role in helping youngsters dress up for Halloween, but they were becoming less central in other ways. In fact, the night itself was increasingly carved up in generational ways. In 1911, a Kingston newspaper reported that it was normal for the smaller children to go street guising between 6 and 7 P.M., visiting shops and neighbors where their rhymes and songs would be rewarded with nuts and candies. Thereafter, the night was reserved for the pranksters, or for the young men and women who dressed up and went off to private dances or parties.[91]

If Halloween was increasingly fashioned as a peer-group festival at the turn of the twentieth century, its symbols and artifacts had become more commercial and standardized. Halloween motifs were regularly displayed in shops, restaurants, and workplaces. These now included the bats and cats, animals not associated with Halloween in the early modern era, despite the well-established links between cats, magic, witchcraft, and devil worship.[92] They seem to have found their way into Halloween lore through nineteenth-century Gothic fiction, most notably, *Varney the Vampire* (1847) and Edgar Allan Poe's *The Black Cat* (1843), stories that were easily adapted for the stage, radio, and silver screen. By the 1920s, bats and cats were as familar to Halloween as witches and goblins, all of which were set in an orange and black or sometimes yellow and black decor. As one instructional booklet from Boston observed, "Decorations for Hallowe'en may vary greatly, but black cats, bats, Jack'o'Lanterns, ghosts and witches predominate. Autumn leaves, corn-stalks, fruits and vegetables carry the idea of a harvest celebration. Orange and black crepe paper are indispensable in decorating."[93]

By the 1920s, there were many ways to celebrate Halloween and many places where that happened outside the home: town halls, church halls, hospitals, schools. For the elite, there were country clubs and mansions, art galleries and hotels, including the Orangery at the Hotel Astor. For those who simply wanted a night out, it was possible to go to the theater to see some Halloween-related show. In 1920, the Kingston Grand Opera House imported the New York production of *Jack O'Lantern*, a musical extravaganza featuring Doyle and Dixon, "America's greatest dancers and comedians."[94] Some 300 Queen's students and some "local youths" attempted a rush on the doors, but they were repulsed by the police. Four of the ringleaders were arrested, fined, and lectured by Magistrate Farrell on what were the bounds of "legitimate fun" on Halloween.[95] As we see later, those boundaries continued to be a source of tension and controversy for much of the century.

☾ 4 ☺

Razor in the Apple

The Struggle for a Safe and Sane Halloween,

c. 1920–1990

If the 1920s saw the emergence of Halloween as a genuinely North American holiday and one that was becoming something of a boon for shopkeepers and manufacturers, there remained the nagging problem of just how wild it would be. The concerns voiced by the *Montreal Gazette* in 1910 about the "unhallowed" character of Halloween were not ones that simply disappeared. In fact, the conventions of rascality that invigorated turn-of-the-century Halloween took a long time to die. While youngsters would dress up in fancy costumes and masquerade in the streets, visiting houses for various treats, their older brothers would indulge in a different kind of devilry. As the *Star* quite casually reported of one small town east of Toronto: "Hallowe'en spirit held full sway in Whitby last night. Many a citizen found his veranda furniture hanging from spikes on telephone poles, while a number of gates were removed and steps taken away."[1] On a typical Halloween spree in interwar North America, fences were destroyed, signs and gates removed, roads barricaded, trolley cars immobilized, street lighting smashed, and outhouses tipped over. One eminent historian of Canada assured me that in his more youthful days in the 1930s he turned over as many as fourteen outhouses in one night of Halloween pranks.

In some places, manhole covers were removed from the streets and fake detour signs put up to harass motorists. Occasionally, traffic signals were tampered with to promote general confusion. Predictably, the new symbol of prosperity, the automobile, became the object of destruction. Revelers soaped windows, deflated tires, and at busy intersections unceremoniously "bounced" cars, or rocked them from the back, to the discomfort of the passengers. In downtown areas, the police were on red alert on Halloween. Sometimes, special reinforcements were brought in to ensure that the jollity of the evening did not degenerate into widespread vandalism. In Winnipeg during the Depression, "mobs of unruly youths and juvenile gangs" habitually gave the cops a "busy night."[2] In 1933, it was reported that there "was a merry game of give and take, the milling mobs retreating and advancing as the pressure of police control surged and receded."[3]

The confrontations between the police and youthful revelers were generally good-natured. There were usually few arrests for damage to property. In 1932, the *Vancouver Sun* reported that the "humor of police officers was frayed by almost two hours' continuous disturbances . . . and yet some of the pranks were so irresistibly funny that even they had difficulty in keeping a serious face."[4] As this quote suggests, the tone of the interwar press was seldom one of outright outrage. The *Winnipeg Free Press* talked of "jollity and hooliganism" or "jollity and horse play" when describing the antics of Halloween, and did not attribute to them any undergirding sense of urban malaise.

When the police did get tough with revelers, there were sometimes protests from the public. In 1936, the jailing of seven small boys who splattered tomatoes over a newly painted veranda in Richmond Hill, just outside of Toronto, led to howls of protests from local residents, who believed that the police had overreacted to what was nothing more than a customary prank.[5] Two years earlier, the citizens of Kerrisdale, Vancouver, were up in arms over what they termed the "buckomate"[6] tactics of the police, who used a mounted force to disperse a Halloween crowd. The police argued that their actions were a legitimate response to the damage caused the previous year, when "a crazy gang of youths" looted stores and dragged automobiles around the block. In fact, residents, including the principal of the local school, had demanded greater vigilance. But this did not stop Clarence Campbell, a thirty-year-old garage man, from suing the police for using excessive force in the dispersal of a customary revel. He had been trampled down in the affray and bore the "souvenirs of blows from a policeman's whip."[7]

As this Vancouver incident suggests, citizens disagreed about how much tolerance should be given to the annual Halloween revel. Some clearly demanded better police protection from Halloween pranksters, for the calls to the stations in cities like Toronto and Vancouver ran into double, even triple figures every year. In rural areas, in particular, where the mayhem on Halloween might seemed especially threatening, a few householders even took the law into their own hands. In 1933, for example, a farmer from Uxbridge, Ontario, fired at pranksters who threw stones on the roof of his house, wounding one of them. In the same year, another farmer from the same district, besieged by a gang of revelers who peppered his farmstead with stones, opened fire repeatedly, wounding five young men aged fifteen to twenty-five years. In Welland, too, where a gang of youths bombarded a home in Cook's Mills with apples as a climax to its Halloween pranks, two men were injured by gunshots in the ensuing affray.[8] Four years later, in Southey, Saskatchewan, a seventy-one-year-old man shot dead one of the pranksters who was pestering him, having repeatedly warned them to leave his property.[9] In isolated rural districts, where rowdies cruised farms in trucks and where farmers had firearms handy, confrontations could be tragically bloody.

Shootings on Halloween made good news copy. So, too, did the tales of fatal accidents and fires that accompanied the pranks of the night. While these stories undoubtedly exaggerated the mayhem of the holiday, they probably reinforced the idea that Halloween had to be tamed and modernized, at least among security-sensitive citizens. This could not be accomplished by the traditional forms of crowd control, for police forces were always stretched to capacity on this annual mischief night. It had to be effected by community groups who strove to channel youthful energies into more respectable, law-abiding activities. All manner of clubs and societies went out of their way to provide alternative events for Halloween. Lions, Rotarians, Kiwanis, religious groups, high schools, boys' and girls' clubs, women's institutes, the Imperial Order of the Daughters of the Empire, and even the Sons of the American Revolution all rose to meet the challenge of rendering Halloween safe and sane during the interwar years.

For the younger set, there were fancy-dress competitions and games. For the adolescents, there were organized dances, usually capped with prizes for the most imaginative costumes. Smaller communities even staged Halloween carnivals or street fairs to deter youths from vandalism. At Independence, Kansas, residents organized a "Neewollah" celebration that featured a parade, musical comedy, and the crowning of an annual Queen. In Anoka, Minnesota, the local Commercial Club and Kiwanis also put on an annual festival and parade on Halloween, beginning in 1920. A few years later, Los Angeles organized a series of carnivals in an effort "to transform the annual celebration from a night of vandalism to one of fun for all."[10] Canadian towns quickly followed suit. In Winnipeg, the United Scottish Association staged an annual carnival at the Minto armories and subsequently at the Winnipeg Auditorium, drawing thousands of merry-makers. In 1938, more than 5000 people were said to have jammed the auditorium, at which there was a six-act vaudeville followed by a fancy-dress contest in which over 200 participated.[11] In Whitby, Ontario, the War Veterans and Citizens' Band organized a Halloween fair in 1928, complete with a masquerade parade, booths, and dancing in local halls and on the street.[12] Other Ontarian towns soon followed, including Shelburne, where the local Rotary Club organized a torchlight parade and a big scramble that was designed to deter children from holding shopkeepers ransom for all manner of goods.[13]

These community-sponsored events were likely quite successful in curbing Halloween revelry in smaller towns and townships; at the very

least, they established acceptable limits of festive license. In the larger
cities, they simply made the task of policing Halloween a little easier
by weaning the more respectable classes from the rougher forms of
Halloween hilarity. But there were still occasions when Halloween
revelry ran out of control. In some cities Halloween gave full vent to
troublesome racial tensions. In 1931 in Nashville, North Carolina,
Halloween masqueraders barred the downtown business district from
"colored folk," savagely beating one black in a minor race riot. Three
years later in New York, 400 revelers armed with stones and stockings
rioted in Harlem, black against white, until the police intervened.[14] In
downtown Vancouver, too, Halloween revels were seldom free from
racial tension during the interwar years, for pranksters habitually
swarmed Chinatown for a "little fun" at the Asians' expense. In 1935,
youth gangs looted a large number of Japanese stores in the central
section of the city. Four years later, 200 youths marched through
Chinatown and the "Japanese colony," shooting off firecrackers and
smashing windows. A similar raid was prevented the following year
only by stationing officers at every corner of the district.[15]

     Even without racial incitement, Halloween revelry could spiral out
of control in North America's larger cities. During the Depression years,
the Halloween custom of holding storekeepers ransom for candies, nuts,
and apples became something of an economic imperative among the
unemployed and their dependents. There was always the possibility that
the holiday would become raucously aggressive. When the Chicago
World's Fair of 1934 ended on 31 October, the authorities should have
predicted trouble. At midnight, some 300,000 revelers, some of them
masked as witches, took complete control of 32 miles of streets and
concessions, "drank everything in sight except Lake Michigan," and
rifled everything "moveable as souvenirs." At the horticultural building,
for example, "thrifty housewives" were reported taking home $200
plants as admission souvenirs. Hundreds of police reserves were brought
in to clear the crowds from the fairground, but crowds were still pouring
in as late as 3 A.M.[16] Some ritual pillaging of the concessions was to be

expected on the last day of the fair; ending it on Halloween undoubtedly invited a general plunder.

If the Chicago authorities were unprepared for what happened in 1934, so, too, were those in Toronto. In the late 1930s, the police found themselves perennially battling pranksters in the West End of the city, particularly those who dropped firecrackers into mailboxes, opened water hydrants, and dragged parked cars into the middle of the street. In 1940, the police department reminded Torontonians that Halloween was for children and that they would crack down on any horseplay by adolescents.[17] This warning appeared to have the desired effect, for in the next few years Halloween was celebrated reasonably quietly, to a point that the *Globe* could feature a homely cartoon in which "junior" fails to frighten his father with a ghostly prank.[18]

The cartoon proved ill timed. In various parts of Toronto and neighboring townships, Halloween was celebrated with unusual exuberance in 1945. In North York, gangs of youths roamed the streets, burning "almost everything they could set afire." In Weston, two men and five juveniles were arrested for maliciously damaging property and placing stumps of trees on the railway tracks.[19] The most spectacular disturbance occurred in Toronto's East End, in the vicinity of Kew Beach. Here high-school kids ignored an invitation to attend the Halloween celebrations organized by a local service club and erected several bonfires on Queen Street East. They fueled these fires with torn-down fences and building materials, adding to the general inferno by spilling gasoline on the streetcar tracks. When the mounted police arrived, the crowd was ordered to disperse. The order was defied. The police were pelted with rocks, and revelers used blocks of concrete from a nearby excavation site to barricade the street from the fire trucks. Thirteen were arrested in the ensuing affray, in which five firemen and two police officers suffered injuries. Yet the riot did not end there. Led by two sailors, an estimated crowd of 7000 "youths and young girls" descended upon the police station on Main Street to rescue the young men who had been detained, turning on fire hydrants along the way.

In the stand-off, police reserves and cruiser cars carrying tear gas rushed to the station, and the "howling mob" was finally dispersed only by water cannon from the fire trucks.[20]

The Kew Beach riot was reckoned to be the worst Halloween disturbance in Toronto's history. Bail for the ringleaders, two of whom were servicemen but most of whom were teenagers, was set at the inordinately high sum of $1000, so most were kept in jail for three weeks before their trials. The majority were given stiff fines. "Halloween has always been a children's night," remarked the *Globe*. "But when the night of innocent fun turns into wild rioting by young men in their late teens and early twenties, then the law must take its course. There is no room for rowdyness—in any community which prides itself on its stability and respect for the property of others."[21] "There is nothing in the 31st of October which makes it an open day for wanton destruction and personal violence," added the *Telegram*. "Nor is there any custom which extends to adolescents and adults the indulgence which winks at childish and harmless pranks on that date or which excuses the lawless behavior of hoodlums and morons."[22]

In framing their indictment of the Kew Beach rioters the Toronto newspapers were, in effect, rewriting the past. Halloween had never been exclusively or even primarily a children's holiday. As befitted a liminal festival, it belonged more properly to those between childhood and adulthood. This was how Robert Burns saw it in his oft cited poem *Hallowe'en*, recognizing its importance to early-modern courtship customs and to social, principally masculine, license. The holiday's appeal in North America stemmed precisely from the temporary freedom that it gave to young people to defy social convention and to seize the streets. Pranks were an important feature of this season of misrule. While they were often aimlessly directed at passers-by, they were also, for better or worse, collective retributions directed against those elements in society who were thought to be alien, snobbish, or antisocial. Certainly, the costuming and games associated with Halloween were easily adapted to the child's imaginary world and became part of a child's socialization with family, friends, and neighborhood. But Halloween did not derive its appeal from these age-specific practices. Although Halloween was occasionally called "Kiddies' Night" in the interwar years, it was very clear that it involved not only the pre-teens but also adolescents.[23] All age groups, in fact, had opportunities to dress up on Halloween and attend dances or parties. Even the festive begging associated with the night was never the exclusive province of children. In 1932, a journalist reported that "a pack of teen-age boys" swept into a confectioner's store "in mass formation" and demanded treats to "yells of 'Shell out.'" Teenage boys and girls besieged Vancouver homes in a similar fashion the following year.[24]

The authorities' answer to these youthful high spirits on Halloween was varied. In July 1950, the Judiciary Committee of the U.S. Senate recommended to President Harry Truman that Halloween should be transformed into a "Youth Honor Day." The resolution was intended "to give national recognition to the efforts of organizations throughout the country which have attempted to direct the activities of young people into less-destructive channels on Halloween day of each year."[25] According to the plan, youngsters would receive pledge cards at school urging them not to destroy property on the holidays. Once this pledge was given, they would receive a ticket to a Halloween dance or party. The plan had been promoted in 1950 by the sheriff of Davenport, Iowa, who hoped it would be adopted by 2000 towns across the United States.[26]

Pledging was one of several ideas for diverting youthful energies in more respectable directions. The National Recreational Association, for example, tried to wean youths from smashing windows and puncturing tires by organizing window painting competitions, costume parties, and visits to other children in hospitals. Here the strategy was to make youngsters "partners in play rather than conspirators in mischief."[27]

This sort of approach had also been recommended by the Toronto authorities in the aftermath of the Kew Beach riot of 1945. "There is much that can be done in the way of community enterprises which will provide a worthy outlet for the exuberance of youth," opined the *Globe*.

It went on to commend the celebration of Halloween at Swansea village in Toronto's West End, where the entertainments were organized according to school age and where there were "no rowdy street scenes" and few "village shell-out calls."[28] Like other newspapers, it was relieved to report that the Halloween rioting of Toronto's East End in 1945 was succeeded in 1946 by a popular party at the Malvern Collegiate high school that attracted thousands of teenagers. It was in the city's best interests that Halloween became more of a dating ritual than an occasion for street rowdiness.

Insofar as rascality could be tolerated at all, it was better that it be rendered child-like. The logic of this argument led inexorably to the trick-or-treat. Originally introduced into North America around 1939 and gaining momentum in the 1950s, trick-or-treating radically altered the dynamics of festive license without eliminating its masking or playful features. Earlier conventions of festive doles always carried with them a heavy weight of social obligation and the threat of recriminatory action if such expectations were not satisfied. Patrons were expected to deliver or, in the imperative of the interwar years, to "shell out." One correspondent to the *Vancouver Sun* remarked that Halloween begging was tantamount to "paying tribute . . . to potential pirate bands by giving largesse at the door."[29] If gifts were not forthcoming, property might be vandalized, although much depended upon local practices. In the Philadelphia area, for example, the threshold treating was sometimes a ritualized reconciliation between householder and youngster in the wake of a week's petty vandalism.[30] Elsewhere property might be vandalized without the ritual of trick-or-treat, for male adolescents often dispensed with such rites in their eagerness to harass an unpopular neighbor. On Halloween, recalled Ray Rheinhart of his boyhood days in Hoboken, New Jersey, just across the Hudson from midtown Manhattan, "there was only mischief. The adult world could not buy us off with candy or shiny pennies. They didn't even try."[31] Instead, he remembered, they braced themselves for the vandalism of "hyper male adolescents who could hardly wait for the sun to go down."

Once it was dark, any metal garbage pail left unsecured was unceremoniously tossed down the stone steps that led to the basements of the city's brick and brownstone row houses. The clatter of metal against concrete usually continued right up to midnight. If there was a cast-iron fence around a property, the gates were likely to be stolen. Of course, clean car windows were targets for the milky scrawls of soap bars.

Gregory Stone remembered detaching the eave troughs from the house of the neighborhood "crab" in the mid-1930s and hurling them "with a terrifying clatter" upon his front porch. He and his friends, he noted, "had no conception of being treated by our victims to anything except silence . . . irate words, a chase (if we were lucky), or, most exciting of all, an investigation of the scene by the police whom we managed to elude."[32] Ironically, some commentators naively thought that if older boys could be induced to visit neighbors' houses for a treat, vandalism would be significantly reduced.[33]

Within this context, trick-or-treating sought to marginalize adolescent pranking and to defuse the antagonism inherent in the festive tribute, transforming the exchange into a rite of consumption. In this new convention of festive doleing, children dressed up and unreflexively requested candies from local neighbors with little sense of what "tricking" might mean. As one observer noted, postwar Halloween, like other national observances, effectively prepared children for mass consumption, for the dominant ethic of the day. In his words, "it was a rehearsal for consumership without a rationale."[34] The holiday became a boon for food manufacturers and retailers, who were always ready to advertise nuts, cookies, and candies in the context of Halloween's door-to-door soliciting, and who had even attempted to introduce a Candy Day to the public calendar.[35] Over time, Halloween became an important night for costumers, as well; for whereas children of the interwar years constructed their costumes from the old clothes in the attic or closet and simply blackened their faces with burnt cork or soot, children in the more affluent 1950s and 1960s were more likely to buy Halloween masks and perhaps other articles of their costume from retail stores. By making Halloween consumer-oriented and infantile, civic and industrial promoters hoped to eliminate its anarchic features. By making it neighborly and familial, they strove to reappropriate public space from the unorthodox and ruffian and restore social order to the night of 31 October.

In practice, the consumerist ethos of the trick-or-treat was often mitigated by its charitable functions. During World War II, Canadian children solicited money for their British counterparts whose homes had been destroyed by the Blitz, under the auspices of the British War Victims' Fund or the Red Cross.[36] This charitable practice was developed in different directions after the war. In 1952, the American Friends (Quakers) Service Committee suggested that Halloween be transformed into a "Friendly Beggars' Night," when trick-or-treaters could collect usable items for poorer children overseas, such as food, clothing, shoes, books, games, or toys.[37] In the wealthy suburb of Grosse Pointe, Michigan, the threshold call of the 1950s was not "Shell out" or "Trick or treat" but "Help the poor."[38]

The idea of linking Halloween to charity caught on. With presidential approval, it was taken up by the newly formed United Nations, which encouraged trick-or-treaters to collect money for their Children's Fund. In 1954, as many as 1500 U.S. communities participated in this "new style Halloween," one that was approvingly reported to have significantly reduced the vandalism of the holiday.[39]

Within a few years, the trickster with the UNICEF (United Nations International Children's Emergency Fund) armband and collection jar was a familiar sight on the doorsteps of North America. In 1956, children from 7500 communities in the United States collected $792,000 for the fund. In the following year, the collection topped $1 million in the United States and $125,000 in Canada.[40] There were a few objectors. In suburban Milwaukee, two Catholic priests banned youngsters in

The wicked witch and bunny trick-or-treat and collect for UNICEF. *Photo by Kate Greenslade.*

their parish from collecting for UNICEF on the grounds that the organization was riddled with Communism.[41] This accusation was vigorously denied by the American branch of UNICEF, and in the end McCarthyism was not allowed to taint a practice that might civilize Halloween. As the *New York Times* observed, the UNICEF program had "converted a day that was often a nuisance into an opportunity for citizenship education through cooperative community-wide effort."[42]

The 1950s saw the taming of Halloween. "Shell out, shell out," remarked the *Toronto Star* quite light-heartedly, "for this is the week of treats or tricks. So light up the pumpkins and be prepared for everything from ghosts to colonial ladies, live bunnies, blackface comediennes and his satanic majesty."[43] Rather than experience real-life shenanigans, children could find them in a Walt Disney cartoon in which Donald Duck plays tricks on his unsuspecting nephews, who seek revenge with the help of Hazel the witch. The cartoonist Carl Bucks translated this story to the comic books, reconciling the well-known bully with his little nephews in a happy denouement to Halloween.[44] This spirit of amity was replicated publicly, for by 1960, much of the mischief formerly associated with the holiday had ebbed. One police sergeant in Los Angeles publicly wondered what had happened to all the juvenile delinquents after a tranquil Halloween in 1959.[45] Of course, it was possible to find some communities where the old traditions of mayhem coexisted with trick-or-treating. In some of the small Irish-Canadian townships south of Ottawa, for example, kids would graduate from the neighborly rounds of the trick-or-treat to the not-so-neighborly pranks of removing the movable, soaping-up windows, and tearing down signs. In Chesterville, every Halloween become a trial of strength between local youths and the police, in which a night in the lock-up became the ultimate adolescent cachet.[46] In some of the older East Coast cities, too, such as Camden, New Jersey, Halloween retained its rougher edge. But in suburban North America, a combination of community-sponsored events, recreational programs, collection for UNICEF, and trick-or-treating, not to mention the rising affluence of the era, went a long way toward taming Halloween.

Within little more than a decade, however, widespread rumors of tampered treats and razors in apples unsettled the equanimity that characterized the holiday. The first tale of tainted candies that hit the news involved a dentist from Centerville, near Fresno, California, who was charged with giving laxatives to sixteen trick-or-treaters.[47] Similar tales of contamination cropped up in the 1960s, peaking in 1970 when the first death attributed to Halloween treats was reported. This involved a five-year-old named Kevin Toston, who died after supposedly eating a heroin-laced candy, although Toston may have picked up the drug from his uncle's house.[48] From then on, stories of candies spiked by "Halloween sadists" began to circulate more widely, sensationalized by news of a second death in 1974. This concerned eight-year-old Timothy O'Bryan, who ate a cyanide-contaminated *Pixie Stix*. Texas prosecutors alleged that Timothy's father, Ronald Clark O'Bryan, had planted the candy in his son's bag of goodies in order to claim the life insurance from his death. When O'Bryan was tried and convicted of capital murder in May 1975, his story made headline news. Although this Halloween fatality was clearly home-based, fears of contaminated candies being handed out to innocent children billowed in the press. In the run-up to Halloween in 1975, *Newsweek* warned Americans to be wary of allowing their children to accept apples or candies, especially if unwrapped or perforated, from strangers. "If this year's Halloween follows form," the weekly asserted, "a few children will return home with something more than just an upset tummy: in recent years, several children have died and hundreds have narrowly escaped injury from razor blades, sewing needles and shards of glass purposefully put into their goodies by adults."⁴⁹

The spectacle of a very sick Halloween was taking shape and was deeply troubling to many people. One observer from Niagara Falls reminisced about safer times:

> Trick or treat. That's all that was heard on Hallowe'en. Every two seconds the door bell would ring and there would stand various kinds of little creatures, bunny rabbits, Franken-steins, hobos, the whole bit. You name it. They were at the door collecting their candy. One little boy came to the door. For a moment there I thought it was a girl. He had on a beautiful wig and make-up on his face. He also had on a long granny gown with two big balloons filling in the top. What struck me funny was that after I had given him the candy his balloons started to pop. Two seconds later he was as flat as a pancake. There were so many other cute little costumes I just could not begin to describe them all. This part of Hallowe'en is the fun part, but just to think that

some sadistic person would try to harm these helpless little children. Just think how great it would be to have Hallowe'en without finding needles, pins, razor blades, dope etc. in their candy bags.[50]

A second major Halloween scare came seven years later, in the wake of the seven deaths from cyanide-laced Tylenol pills in September 1982, and the scheduled execution of Ronald O'Bryan on Halloween for the murder of his son. This time the panic reached crisis proportions. The Associated Press reported 175 alleged incidents of candy tampering on Halloween in 1982, in as many as 100 cities. The U.S. Food and Drug Administration listed over 270 such incidents from the time that the Tylenol scandal broke. Of these, only thirty-six revealed "hardcore, true tampering" in the department's estimation, but the rumors of Halloween sadists on the loose was enough to sap public confidence in the holiday. Candy manufacturers spent $400,000 that year in an attempt to dispel public anxiety, joining the campaign for a safe and sane Halloween and encouraging hospitals to provide radiology units to X-ray treats. Despite these efforts, public participation in trick-or-treating declined dramatically. Many U.S. towns banned the practice altogether, while others imposed strict curfews. Candy sales dropped by 20 percent or more.[51]

Canadians, too, were caught up in the panic over tainted candies. The Tylenol poisonings had been widely covered on television, with the result that parents were especially vigilant in inspecting candies when Halloween came around. In most cities across the country, trick-or-treating declined dramatically, by as much as 50 percent in some suburbs in the Vancouver area.[52] Several incidents of contaminated treats were reported, over and above the stories of razors in apples that the police routinely received. These included lye-dusted chewing gum and poisoned candies in Ottawa and pins and small nails in candies in Halifax.[53] No serious casualties were reported, and no municipalities within Canada appear to have insisted upon banning Halloween or establishing curfews. All the same, as a note given to a child in Montreal declared, "As you are most likely aware, Halloween is not the same anymore."[54]

Virtually everywhere, the search began for alternative modes of celebrating the holiday. These included school and church-sponsored parties, shopping mall crawls in which celebrants could redeem their
Halloween coupons at specified stores, group visits to spook houses, and
simulated horror shows at museums, zoos, and community centers. In
1984, as many as 108 recreational centers in Washington, D.C., scheduled Halloween festivities as an alternative to trick-or-treating.[55] The
practice of trick-or-treating at neighbors' houses, did revive after 1982,
but on a diminished scale. A 1985 poll reported that only 60 percent of
all parents with children under fifteen were planning to take them trick-
or-treating, even on a restricted round to friends and close neighbors.[56]
The days of the ubiquitous trick-or-treat appeared to be over.

Since only two deaths and relatively few injuries have been reported
from the tampering with Halloween treats, it might be tempting to
suggest that the new era of Halloween sadism was simply a product
of media hype. Certainly, the media played an important role in dis-
seminating the news of the O'Bryan murder and noting its
conjunction with the Tylenol scare eight years later. It also helped to
shape the discourse of Halloween "sadism," even though it was sometimes done playfully, if not ironically, as was the case with Sydney
Schanberg's short article in the New York Times entitled "Era of the
New Sadism."[57] Yet the media did not fabricate the panic so much as
fan it. The role of the press, in particular, was opportunistic and
contradictory, relaying unconfirmed reports of candy tampering while
discounting their wide incidence. Given the often open-ended and
summary manner in which this reportage was cast, the press likely fed
rumors of candy tampering that were already circulating through
informal channels. These rumors often centerd on the razor-in-the-
apple syndrome rather than upon more life-threatening chemical
pollutants, at least after 1966, when the concern for safe trick-or-
treating began to attract wide public attention.[58]

Sociologists and folklorists have described the belief in Halloween
sadism as an "urban legend."[59] As with other urban legends, this one
had some factual basis, but the fears it generated were disproportionate

to the confirmed cases of candy contamination. The National Confectioners Association, for example, reported that of the 90 reported
cases of tampered treats that came to its notice in 1974, the year of the
O'Bryan homicide, 27 were proven hoaxes, 22 were likely ones, and a
further 40 simply evaporated after the original complaint.[60] Without
doubt, the association had its own reasons to discount the rumors, but
in 1982, when the Tylenol poisonings deluged the news networks, public
fears of tainted treats generated what one Food and Drug Administration official termed a bout of "psychosomatic mass hysteria."[61]
Halloween sadism, in fact, spoke more compellingly to the urban
anxieties of the era than to anything else, at least in the United States.
In this respect it is important to understand the changing urban context
that allowed stories of Halloween sadism to flourish.

Tales of Halloween sadism, I have suggested, were measured against
the vision of a stable, congenial decade of trick-or-treating in the 1950s.
This was a decade of Cold War politics and Red scares. Yet beyond the
zone of leftist agitation, it was also a decade of relative social peace, of
a continuing baby boom, of consumer affluence and suburban development. The 1960s and 1970s, however, posed new challenges to the social
and political fabric of the United States. This was the era of civil rights
agitation, of urban ghetto riots, of student and antiwar protest, of youth
countercultures, of feminism and gay liberation, of Watergate. In the
South, African-Americans defeated Jim Crow, but in the North they
faced de facto resegregation as whites fled to the suburbs in the wake
of rioting in Watts, Newark, and Detroit. When he came to power in
1963, Lyndon B. Johnson envisaged a "Great Society" that would end
poverty and racial injustice. But the war on poverty was stalled by
Vietnam and a refusal to confront the existing structures of power and
wealth. And racial justice proved illusory while there was systemic
discrimination against blacks.

In an address at the University of Michigan in 1964, Johnson declared
that "our society will never be great until our cities are great."[62] Yet ten
years on, many cities seemed like smoldering cauldrons of despair and

violence. Homicide rates soared, reaching an all-time high of 10.7 per 100,000 in 1980.[63] Youth crime, much of it drug- or gang-related, rose dramatically. With this came a deepening perception that American cities were no longer safe places in which to live. A 1974 opinion poll in New York State revealed that inhabitants saw crime, drugs, and law and order as among the three most important problems facing the country. Some 55 percent of those interviewed said that "they worried a lot about walking alone in the streets after dark." In New York City, the figure was as high as 71 percent, but even in leafy Westchester and further upstate, figures of 45 and 43 percent were recorded.[64]

At the same time, there was a growing mistrust of strangers among urban dwellers, a loss of neighborhood solidarity, and a fear that children were increasingly vulnerable to child abuse and molestation. This fear was often associated with the fact that an increasing number of mothers were in the workforce outside of home. In the United States in 1970, the proportion of married mothers with children under eighteen who worked full time was 16 percent; the proportion who worked part-time was as high as 51 percent.[65] Combined with the growing number of single-parent families, there was a billowing concern about the safety of unsupervised, latch-key kids.

These anxieties predictably dovetailed with those associated with Halloween. The first major holiday of the school year, and one in which children were conventionally on the streets after dark, it was a prime opportunity for child abuse. Although the two deaths associated with Halloween may have involved family members, the threat of anonymous malice loomed large. "In many cities now," Benjamin Stein asserted in the *Washington Post*,

> children are given apples with needles in them, candy bars with razor blades inside, chewing gum with LSD. Children go out treating and never come home. Instead of warnings about eating too much, children get warnings to taste nothing until they get home, to speak to no one, to accept

no rides from anyone, and, above all in this year of awareness
of child sexual abuse, to let no adult touch them.[66]

Fright night could take ominous turns, even in the seemingly safe
suburbs. It only took only a few stories about candy-tampering to vitiate
the tradition of trick-or-treating. As Catherine Ainsworth's respondents
in Niagara Falls testified, such stories were rife. "I'm sad to report that
I handed candy out to only seventy-five children this year," reported
Julie Lucas in 1972.

> Last year we had the pleasure of three hundred of the little
> ones out for fun. The reason for the decline is probably due
> to a few warped minds who killed or badly hurt them last
> year with razor blades and drugs. The tykes remained on
> their own blocks this year and more mothers came with
> them to protect them. I feel it is a shame that these tiny
> people have to miss out on one of the great joys of
> childhood, that most of us loved so much.[67]

While Niagara Falls residents were bemoaning the decline of the
trick-or-treat, Halloween was taking a more ominous turn in downtown
Detroit. In the late 1970s and 1980s, Detroit was the scene of widespread
conflagrations on Halloween and the subject of considerable publicity
in the American and international press. In fact, Detroit's Halloween
season became so unruly, so full of arson, that civil reputations were
staked on trying to control it. Why this happened requires a brief detour
into Detroit's industrial and racial history.

As one of the leading centers of the automobile industry, Detroit
was for many years an American success story. In the early decades of
the twentieth century, thousands of European and Canadian immigrants
flocked to the city, found jobs, and integrated themselves into what was
a workable urban mosaic dominated by an Anglo-American elite.[68]
When blacks ventured north from the Mississippi Delta, however, they
faced severe discrimination over housing and jobs. Rioting broke out

Scorching the town, a cartoon on Detroit's Devil's Night, 1991. *Reprinted with permission of the* Detroit Free Press.

over housing allocations in the 1920s and again in 1942, when white picketers attempted to prevent blacks from moving into the federally funded Sojourner Truth project. In the following year, white and black gangs squared off against one another at the Belle Island amusement park. This confrontation escalated into a full-scale invasion of black neighborhoods and further violence, which in turn led to police and military intervention and a death toll of thirty-four. Twenty-six of the victims were African-Americans.[69]

Racial tensions eased during the 1950s but resumed their former intensity in the following decade. Detroit experienced a further spate of rioting, the most serious incident occurring in 1967, when a police raid on an after-hours club in the black section of town led to rumors of police brutality. Crowds gathered and smashed stores, and in the bloody conflict that ensued, forty-three people were killed, most of them from gunshots by the police and the national guard.

Confrontations such as this one led whites to abandon the inner city in increasing numbers. In fact, for the majority of whites, the 1967 riots signaled that Detroit was "beyond the point of no return."[70] The city's downtown population declined during the 1960s, while that of the surrounding suburbs rose by 32 percent. By 1970, Detroit had a population of 1.4 million, compared with 2 million in 1950, at the peak of its power and influence. As commerce joined whites in fleeing the city,[71] Detroit was on its way to becoming a predominantly black city with high levels of unemployment: 26 percent in 1970 and even higher levels among adolescent blacks aged sixteen to nineteen (31 percent). According to the 1970 census, nearly 19 percent of all families were below the poverty line, while 15 percent were on public assistance.

Two things happened to make Detroit's situation quite desperate. First, the auto industry went into serious decline in the face of foreign competition, corporate reorganization, and plant cutbacks. Between 1978 and 1986, Detroit lost virtually a third of its jobs in the auto industry. Second, the tax base of the city plummeted to dangerously low levels. This made it very difficult for the urban authorities to sustain the levels of public housing that the inner-city population required. In fact, because the state of Michigan banned deficit budgets, it made it impossible to mount massive public works programs to bring hope and jobs to the unemployed. Deindustrialization and neoconservative economics was turning Detroit into an urban nightmare. Racism was rife, vandalism commonplace, and a shocking two slayings a day in the mid-1970s turned the "Motor City" into the "Murder City."[72]

The nightmare was visibly evident every Devil's Night. The night before Halloween, Devil's Night is when the seasonal mischief began in what was often a three-night spree in industrial Michigan. That spree did not give rise to the usual repertoire of pranks that characterized Halloween. Like other urban wastelands and areas of industrial decline—Flint, Michigan; Camden, New Jersey; Bell County, Kentucky, to mention but three—Detroit specialized in fires. Fires in trash cans, dumpsters, and in abandoned buildings. And in Detroit, there were houses to spare as families simply packed up and left. In the fiscal year 1989–90 alone, the city tore down nearly 5000 abandoned homes as a prelude to a rebuilding program.[73]

Fires on the three nights around Halloween started to reach alarmingly high levels in the early 1980s, but in 1983 they skyrocketed. In that year, if one includes the 150 fires that purportedly went unreported, the number reached 1000. In 1984, it fell only slightly, to 840. City ordinances imposing curfews between 10 P.M. and 6 A.M. for youths under eighteen attempted to curb the arson during Halloween, but it was claimed that the police seldom enforced them.[74] In 1986, the mayor of Detroit, Coleman Young adopted a tougher strategy. He passed an emergency curfew from dawn to dusk and threatened to bring all violators to juvenile court. At the same time, he mobilized a city watch of 5600 city employees and an equivalent number of volunteers to supplement the 11,000 strong police force. A huge number of flyers were distributed to encourage adolescents to stay off the streets and refrain from raising hell. "Devil's Night is no joke," ran one couplet, "When your house and your ride go up in smoke."[75]

About 750 minors, of whom over 90 percent were male, were arrested during the Halloween season in 1986. The final toll of fires dropped to 360, down from 479 the previous year. In subsequent years, with a larger posse of volunteers and an Adopt-a-House program, Young managed to reduce the number of fires to below 300 for the three nights of Detroit's Halloween. Even so, these efforts were insufficient to dispel Devil's Night's reputation as an evening of fire. Fire buffs flocked from far afield to watch the flames. Cameramen even flew in from Japan to televise the event. And an Israeli author named Ze'ev Chafets, who had been present at Devil's Night in 1987 and knew the area from his youth, described Detroit as a drug-ridden, arson-happy American Beirut in a best-selling exposé of Mo'town.[76] This depiction drew howls of protest from local leaders, who felt that Chafets's negative portrayal of the city's black administration would only fuel racist arguments that African-Americans could not manage the complexities of urban government. Yet Chafets did colorfully capture many of the symptoms of Detroit's social and economic disintegration and the struggle of its black churches to confront the chaos with some dignity, even if he ultimately failed to analyze the causes of the city's decline.

Those underlying causes were summarized by Kirk Cheyfitz in his review of Chafets's book in the *Detroit Free Press*. "Detroit is in a mess. No argument," he admitted.[77]

> But the problem here is not uniquely Detroit's. The problem is the rapid deindustrialization of America—a lack of jobs, a lack of hope and the surfeit of drugs. The problem is one of national policy involving the international flight of American jobs and capital, the growing gap between rich and poor, and the resurgence of racism in a time of economic hardship. The problem is manifest is every major city in the country. It may make Ze'ev Chafets, the *New York Times* and many others feel better to turn Detroit into the hobgoblin of urban America, but, even at Halloween, that myth won't wash.

This review appeared on Devil's Night, 1990, and the fires were lit before the ink was proverbially dry. In fact, the downward trend in arson was reversed that year, with 281 fires reported in the three-day period, as opposed to 223 in 1989. Detroit's Halloween continued to register the alienation and anomie of its inner-city youth. Not citizen mobilizations, nor mass policing, nor the continuing demolition of potential Halloween targets eliminated the devilry. They simply mitigated a situation that had threatened to engulf whole sections of Detroit in flames. And Detroit was not the only city under siege on Halloween: Flint chalked up more than 140 fires in 1989; Camden, 168, two years later.

What the 1980s did, metaphorically, was to take the Norman Rockwell out of Halloween. The vision of a safe and satisfying holiday, in which children could trick-or treat in their own neighborhoods without fear or danger and with minimal supervision, had gone for good. Razors in apples and inner-city devilry revealed a darker, troublesome side of Halloween in the decades after 1970. Trick-or-treating would survive, but in more regulated forms and under a different set of expectations.

In the 1970s, then, Halloween became a parable of urban anxiety in North America. Its so-called malaise was predicated upon a stable and predictable performance of Halloween whose central motif was the "trick or treat" and whose central actor was the child of perhaps 6–12 years old; that is, a pre-teenager. This was the critical referent from which Halloween's "degeneracy" was assessed, just as Halloween's "rowdyism" in the nineteenth century was measured against Burn's bucolic, pastoral vision of the holiday and its rich repertoire of superstitions and pastimes. It is important to recognize this, because both referents were viewed quite reverentially, with more than a little nostalgia. Indeed, like many other social problems of the 1970s and 1980s, Halloween was viewed against the backdrop of an idyllically constructed 1950s, with low divorce rates, stable heterosexual unions, stay-at-home moms, low ethnic and racial tensions, and safe suburbias.

Halloween in the 1950s was probably never as safe or comforting as its later critics presumed. In the *Winnipeg Free Press* of 1950, for example, there is certainly a yearning for the safe and familiar rituals of Halloween. One photograph depicts a boy wistfully peering into a lighted jack-o'-lantern. "Who knows what he sees in old pumpkin face?" the caption asks.

> Something a bit scary, maybe—hints of black cats and the swoosh of witches careening through the air. Something exciting, too—the prospect of going out with the gang for Hallowe'en apples, of fooling the neighbours with a costume and mask, of being allowed out after dark for once. Spooks and hobgoblins, gypsies and pirates, ghosts in second-best sheets—they'll be young and not very frightening, but the world is theirs tonight.[78]

Well, not quite. On the following day, in a review of the evening's antics, the *Free Press* depicted a group of "Gallopin' Ghosts" who had paraded through town on horseback. And while the newspaper chirpily reported that "smashed windows, ripped-up sidewalks, overturned garbage cans and outhouses were at a minimum," it took for granted that "no Hallowe'en would be complete without soaped windows and bonfires in the street."[79] Not to mention the swell of water from the seventy-five hydrants that Halloween jokesters had turned on in a routine night of mayhem.

Halloween had always had its rougher side, and one which city authorities, schools, and church associations had sought desperately to contain in the interwar years. In the 1950s and 1960s these rougher pastimes were brought under some semblance of control, although they were never entirely eliminated from urban street culture. They were part and parcel of the peer-driven Halloween of youthful males who were too old for the rituals of treat-or-treat and uninterested in the seasonal dance or costume party.

If the Halloween of the 1950s still had its rougher edges, it was nonetheless based on tangible social reciprocities within neighborhoods, whether those involved threshold hospitalities or pranks. In the late 1960s and 1970s, as cities came to be seen as unsafe, inhospitable places of unresolved racial and social tensions, the character of Halloween changed, for children and their parents, and also for young adults. It no longer became possible to think of Halloween as having a stable set of rituals and festive expectations. Halloween after 1970 increasingly registered the pulse and identity politics of different Americas: suburban against inner-city, mainstream against ethnic, evangelical against permissive, heterosexual against gay. But before we examine these developments, we must address how Halloween was handled in America's major growth industry, the motion picture. What did the horror film, in particular, have to offer Halloween? How did it affect its meaning and cultural configurations?

⚜ 5 ⚘

HALLOWEEN
GOES to HOLLYWOOD

In 1991, the Grand Rapids Jaycees organized a Halloween party in a refurbished Grand Trunk locomotive on seven miles of railroad between Coppersville and Marne in Michigan. On what was called the "Terror Train," visitors were subjected to scary, live thrills from "horrific actors" during the hour-long trip. The photos in the *Detroit Free Press* depicted a gruesome young man wielding a chainsaw and a waitress offering guests a pizza topped with a rat, bat, and spiders.[1] What is noteworthy about these scenarios is that they were all derived from Hollywood movies. In the gruesome young man, the frightened teenagers might have recognized Leatherface from the *Texas Chain Saw Massacre* (1974); in the rat-topped pizza, an adaptation of a scene from *Whatever Happened to Baby Jane?* (1962), a vintage horror movie starring Bette Davis and Joan Crawford. Even the name of the train itself had a Hollywood referent: *Terror Train* (1979), one of a slew of un-distinguished splatter films in which women are preyed upon by psychopathic murderers.

No one thought the Jaycees were doing the public a disservice in putting on this grisly performance, save conceivably the followers of the Christian fundamentalist Right, who deplore the mobilization of motifs that encourage Satanism and the glorification of evil. Putting on a horror show has become a constituent part of modern Halloween. As the small-town sheriff remarked in the first *Halloween* movie (1978), "Everyone's entitled to one good scare" on a holiday known as Fright Night. Boo zoos and haunted houses provided this service for children. Heavy metal bands in the Alice Cooper tradition did so for teenagers and young adults. Indeed, Cooper himself, in his staged comeback at Detroit on Halloween, 1987, after six years off the touring circuit, promised more "gore" and "buckets of blood" than ever before.[2] And for those of the older set who prefer to savor their Halloween camp in boozier surroundings, there are countless bars and restaurants ready to cater to their taste. At Gretsky's, one of Toronto's thriving downtown sports bars, patrons could watch the *Rocky Horror Picture Show* on Halloween in 1994 while their ears were blasted by music from the "Count"—not Count Basie, one suspects, but, rather, a Dracula-clad band that hopefully drew applause rather than blood.

Quite ironically, the quest for the scary thrill intensified in the wake of the Tylenol scares and the rumors of Halloween sadism. Boo zoos and haunted houses, for instance, were initially promoted by charity groups as an alternative to trick-or-treating or, in Detroit and Camden, to the escalating incidence of arson. "Once they're seven or eight, most children truly enjoy the 'safe scare'—fake blood, vampires, Dracula teeth, shrieks and clanks, Frankenstein, bats in the belfry, and monsters in the basement," remarked one child development specialist, who believed that by that age they could differentiate "what's real" from "what's fantasy."[3] By the 1980s, community centers across North America were converting their premises into temporary haunted houses, where children could wander through a chamber of fears and a tunnel of no return and encounter eerie ghouls or the more familiar monsters of the movie picture industry. Alternatively, people could savor the spooky sanctuaries of city parks, where they would be thrilled by the sudden appearances of ghosts, witches, and Dracula himself. In the advertisements for children's Halloween events in the Washington, D.C., area for 1984, at least a third mentioned haunted houses, barns, or "ghostly

Young Dracula, Montreal, 1998. *Photo by Kate Greenslade.*

gambols."[4] The popularity of these ventures was such that entrepreneurs quickly cashed in, recognizing the market for both children and teenagers. Firms such as Nightscape Productions, Haunted Hayrides Incorporated, and Elm Street Hauntrepreneurs embarked on a "scare-for-profit" enterprise that rivaled that of the community centers and charitable societies by 1991. In that year there were an estimated 1000 to 2000 haunted houses on offer for Halloween.[5] Normally open for two to three weeks, these commercial ventures could each attract as many as 40,000 visitors during the witching season.[6]

Haunted houses are not the only sites of simulated terror that now characterize Halloween. Before their appearance came the movie theater. Precisely when the cinema became a venue for ghostly or grisly Halloweens is unclear. Despite the growing popularity of the horror genre in the 1930s, there is no evidence that it was closely linked to

Halloween in the manner it is today. In the days of homemade costumes, revelers did not draw upon the stock characters from the early horror genre, whether Dracula, Frankenstein's monster, the Mummy, or King Kong. They were more likely to emulate Charlie Chaplin or Mae West than Universal Pictures' monsters. Nor was there any disposition to synchronize the opening of horror films with the witching season. Tod Browning's *Dracula* (1931), starring Bela Lugosi as the blood-sucking Count, came out on Valentine's Day. It was advertised as "The Strangest Love Story of All," probably because of the story's subversive play on sexual pleasure.[7] It was not rerun on Halloween, despite the fact that Bram Stoker's novel had a calendrical sense of foreboding, with Jonathan Harker first meeting the predatory Count on a day when "all the evil things in the world will have full sway."[8] Nor were any of the other horror classics rereleased at the end of October. Halloween parties in the 1930s might occasionally feature tales from the high Victorian Gothic, but the accent of most of them was on Halloween hilarity, not horror.

There were signs of a change in the late 1930s. Orson Welles's radio production of H. G. Wells's *The War of the Worlds* was broadcast on the night before Halloween in 1938. Transferring the locale of the 1898 novel from Britain to the United States, and presenting the story as a series of news bulletins interrupting a musical program, Welles generated frissons of fear throughout North America and a mass panic in New Jersey.[9] From then on, the commercial possibilities of promoting the scary and the macabre on Halloween became more likely. Anthony Boucher's short story on Halloween in 1945, which blended the spooky scenario of Halloween with the literary convention of *noir*, referred to a "Halloween horror bill" at the Campus theater in Berkeley, California. *Shock* comics rendered Halloween horrific in 1950, with the skinflint master of an orphan's asylum getting his comeuppance as a hollowed-out pumpkin. EC comics followed suit with further scenarios of grisly dismemberments.[10] But the advent of the Comic Code Authority in 1954 ended these ventures, with sci-fi and fantasy replacing

FOR...SHEER, STARK HORROR, READ THIS TERRIFYING TALE... GUARANTEED TO JAR YOU OUT OF YOUR SEAT!

HALLOWEEN!

A HORROR SuspenStory   GHASTLY

Halloween horror, from *Shock* comics, 1952.

tales from the crypt. The result was that Halloween was not indelibly associated with horror in the 1950s, and certainly not with the Gothic mode of horror that engaged anxieties associated with cultural loathing or the repressed. In the Toronto area in 1958, the best that the television could offer was *Whispering Ghosts* with Milton Berle and *Footlight Serenade* with Betty Grable and Victor Mature. As for the cinema, viewers could watch adaptations of Tennessee Williams and Ernest Hemingway, but not of Mary Shelley, Edgar Allan Poe, or Bram Stoker.[11] A decade later, horror movies were definitely part of the seasonal fare, but not emphatically so. Television channels scheduled *Frankenstein* with Boris Karloff, and Vincent Price in *The House on the Haunted Hill*. But the biggest scare at the cinema was *Wait Until Dark*, starring Audrey Hepburn. *Rosemary's Baby*, the film that brought the devil right back in the family, actually opened in Toronto on 1 November 1968,[12] close enough to Halloween perhaps, but not in the run-up to fright night itself.

It was in the 1970s and beyond that horror really became the dominant cinematic genre at Halloween. By then, movie-viewers not only could venture to the cinema for "horrorathons," they could watch a fair variety of horror classics and new productions on their TV sets. In the run-up to Halloween in 1986, for example, one journalist noted that at least sixteen horror movies had been aired over the networks in the Washington area, while the "concentration of film nightmares" in other cities was "even more intense."[13] Prominent among them was George Romero's *Night of the Living Dead* (1969), a horror classic about flesh-eating ghouls that was now in the public domain and could be shown without anybody paying for it. Around Washington it was shown on Baltimore's channel 54, Washington's channel 5, public TV channels 22 and 56, and via WOR from New York. One journalist deplored the fact that it was aired in what had previously been known as the "family hour" and with color added, so that the rivers of blood ran red. "Adults may find the film preposterous camp," Tom Shales opined, "but to children, its explicit scenes of cannibals on a rampage can be highly unsettling." Because the Federal Communications Commission had all but relinquished its control of broadcasting to the marketplace, he complained, the living dead were able to "march through prime time in the name of making a buck."

Shales's focus upon *Night of the Living Dead* was not accidental, even allowing for its availability in the public domain, for Romero's film is widely regarded as a turning point in the horror genre. Whereas the horror classics were either set in the past or featured monsters that tended to originate from outside America, such as King Kong or Godzilla, the post-1968 films tended to be rooted in contemporary everyday life.[14] And whereas the early horror movies frequently witnessed the defeat of the menace at the hands of efficacious male experts, post-1968 monsters were often defeated only temporarily, if at all. Indeed, these monsters maraud their victims in an implacable fashion and often slash their bodies both mercilessly and graphically. In Hitchcock's famous stabbing-in-the-shower scene in *Psycho* (1960), the horror of the action comes from the surprise, from the looming menace of the assailant, and from Janet Leigh's desperate attempts to fend off the killer. Only one fleeting shot shows the body actually being stabbed. In the post-1968 movies, the violence is far more graphic and visceral, heightened by more sophisticated special effects. As film critic Isabel Pinedo has remarked: "Gore—the explicit depiction of dismemberment, evisceration, putrefaction, and myriad other forms of boundary violations with copious amounts of blood—takes center stage."[15] That much of the violence is directed against women, whose abject faces of terror are dwelt on in some detail, only heightens the controversy surrounding this new genre of horror.

These slasher films, as they have sometimes been called, have been almost universally condemned in the mainstream press for their glorification of violence, their misogyny, and their sadistic voyeurism. Their popularity has given rise to a good deal of apprehension about their influence on the younger generation, particularly male adolescents, who constitute a large part of their audience.[16]

The only critics who have attempted to redeem this disreputable genre, or at the very least to reassess its cultural significance, have been academics. They have noted, in what is the crux of their analyses, that while the horror genre is principally aimed at the arousal of bodily sensation—the scary thrill, shiver, chill, or shudder—it is also related to the problem of fear *and* loathing. If we are invited to identify with the victims of the horror drama, knowing the predicament they face or are about to confront, we also have to come to terms with the monster. This antagonist is not simply physically fearsome (sometimes he/it is not), it is in some measure abnormal or disgusting. Monsters inspire revulsion. They are cognitively threatening because they breach the norms of ontological or cultural propriety.[17] Monsters represent the

Other; in Freudian or neo-Freudian terms, they are the repressed Other, our collective nightmares. If we move beyond the visceral physicality of the horror movie with its rivulets of blood to contemplate the Other, we can begin to frame an analysis around the dread of difference, to echo the title of a recent book on the genre. Horror movies, despite their low reputation among mainstream critics, can illuminate the raging contradictions within our society, or so the argument runs.[18] Horror is a coded language that enables authors and invites their audiences to explore their fears, hidden desires, and anxieties. These comments are of some pertinence to the horror movies that focus upon Halloween.

Halloween is not simply the principal occasion in the year for broadcasting horror movies; it has also been the subject of horror movies or, at the very least, their narrative's setting. Indeed, while film directors have often situated their horrors in other festive settings such as Valentine's Day, April Fool's Day, Mother's Day, Christmas, or Thanksgiving, Halloween has been the most popular holiday for horror plots. At least ten horror films have revolved around the holiday since 1978, of which the *Halloween* cycle itself has been the most significant.

The association of Halloween with the supernatural, with darkness, decay, and death, is alluded to in these movies. It is often historically inaccurate and hackneyed. *Night of the Demons* (1987) portrays Halloween as a night of supernatural possession, precipitating the elimination of horny young men at the hands of their demonic girlfriends in what is little more than a clichéd romp around a haunted house. Its sequel (1994) is as predictable, with sexually precocious teenagers mixing their seasonal shenanigans with a touch of black magic and falling captive to predatory demons from the haunted Hull House up the road. *Halloween 2* (1981) refers to the bloody rites of Samhain, to the sacrifices of the first-born that are part of Irish lore, but only as incidental graffiti. *Halloween 6* (1995) develops this theme a little further, in that Jaimie Lloyd's baby is cast as the potential victim of an ancient sacrifice to the Lord of the Dead. Marked with the sign of the thorn, she becomes a quarry for both the satanic members of the hospital in which her mother was housed and also for her psychotic relative, Michael Myers. This certainly complicates the chase and allows Myers the opportunity of exacting revenge upon those members of the psychiatric community who had incarcerated him in the previous *Halloween* movies. Yet the "Druidic curse" that periodically settles upon characters in the *Halloween* cycle remains little more than an embellishment to a contemporary serial killer's stalking of his prey.

The single exception is *Halloween 3* (1982), the only film in the cycle that explores the sacrificial aspects of Halloween in a sustained manner. The plot revolves around a crazed Irish entrepreneur named Conal Cochran, who establishes the Silver Shamrock toy factory in a rural Northeastern community specializing in Halloween jokes and masks. In this "season of the witch," to parody the subtitle of the film, Cochran concocts a diabolical plan to eliminate children by placing life-threatening chips from Stonehenge's Blue Stone into Halloween masks that were programmed to explode at 9 P.M. on Halloween. Cochran's decision to inflict mass infanticide upon unsuspecting Halloween children is inspired by a mission to reenact Samhain's ancient rite of "controlling the environment" in order to promote a more robotic future for commerce and manufacture. Precisely why he wished to eliminate his own market for toys remains unclear. Unless his Silver Shamrock factory faced a crisis of overproduction, the decision is oddly irrational, to say the least. Perhaps Cochran's astrological obsessions or psychotic hatred of children overrode his business sense.[19]

Halloween 3 was commercially the least successful of the cycle. Alongside its historical hocus-pocus and incoherence, it lacked the innovative camera work of John Carpenter and his emulators. What made the first *Halloween* such a resounding success was Carpenter's frequent use of the unmounted first-person camera to represent the killer's point of view.[20] In this film and its sequels, viewers were often invited to adopt the murderer's assaultive gaze and to hear his heavy breathing and plodding footsteps as he stalked his prey. These I-camera shots were sometimes replaced by one in which the camera is situated more ambiguously, located slightly behind or to the side of the victimizer, so that part of the killer occupied the foreground of the frame while the potential victim, unaware of any threat, occupied the background. Sometimes this perspective is reversed. The potential victim occupies the foreground, unaware of the killer's lurking presence elsewhere, which is fleetingly disclosed in a mirror, a window, or behind a bush. The sequence of shots is unsettling, heightening the imminence of the threat.

Halloween (1978) was the first of the slasher films in which victims were very consciously and deliberately stalked and in which the subjective camera implicates the viewer in the murderous enterprise. It was also the first to bring stalking closer to home. To a greater degree than either *Night of the Living Dead* or the *Texas Chain Saw Massacre*, both set in the wastelands of rural America, *Halloween* was situated in a familiar setting: a typical, small Midwest town called Haddonfield, Illinois. The opening scene is Halloween, 1963, when all small boys and girls should be out trick-or-treating. The exception to this rule is eight-year-old Michael Myers, who, dressed in a clown's costume, has been neglected by his sister, in whose care he has been consigned. She is making out with her boyfriend upstairs, a sexual encounter that Michael confronts by taking her life once the boyfriend has departed. The scene then shifts to 1978, when Michael escapes from a psychiatric institution to return to Haddonfield with the intention of killing his younger sister (Laurie Strode) and, as it happens, her sexually active friends. The sequels more or less repeat the narrative formula. Myers returns on Halloween to reenact the trauma of 1963, seeking to eliminate the surviving members of his immediate family and their friends, and those who happen to frustrate his quest.

Halloween was initially conceived as a film about a homicidal maniac who kills babysitters. It had little relation to the actual holiday beyond a desire to cash in on spooky effects and to capitalize upon the relative paucity of films between summer and Christmas, outside the film festival market.[21] Yet the use of the holiday as the site for Myers's homicidal

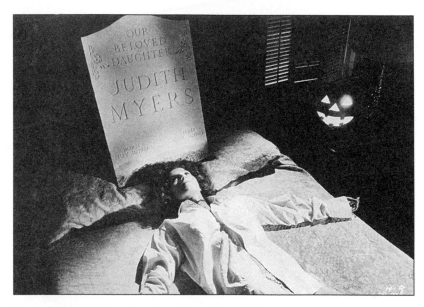

One of Michael Myers's early victims, from *Halloween*.

rage is not simply opportunistic. It has some relevance to the narratives of the Halloween cycle. Quite apart from the link to the 1963 tragedy, Halloween facilitates Myers's elusiveness and the vulnerability of his victims by virtue of the fact that it is a night for masks and pranks. Although Myers briefly emulates a ghost in the first *Halloween*, when he accosts and kills Laurie's friend Annie Brackett, he normally appears wearing a white mask stolen from a store and the working clothes of a garage mechanic. This is a familiar enough disguise to allow Myers to elude detection. In fact, in two sequels other people wearing the same costume are mistakenly taken for him. This confusion is amplified by the general activities of the night. False alarms and hoaxes stretch the resources of the police to the limit and blur the distinction between scary thrills and genuine calls for help. Parents drift off to their own parties, leaving their children at the potential mercy of Myers's murderous schemes. Teenagers are largely left to their own devices, and sometimes resent the responsibilities of taking their younger siblings

Halloween 5: The Revenge of Michael Myers.

on to go trick-or-treating. In *Halloween 4* (1988), Rachel is given charge of her stepsister, Jaimie (Myers's niece), wrecking her own plans for the night with her boyfriend Brady. As a result of their contretemps, Jaimie is left at large, wandering the streets in a clown costume identical to that worn by Michael Myers in the original *Halloween* prologue, with Myers himself predictably in pursuit.

Halloween thus creates a critical space for Myers's sanguinary ventures. But it also exploits the bogeymen myth of Halloween lore. Although Myers's own character is never adequately developed in *Halloween* and its sequels, two explanations for his murderous rage come into play. The first is psychological: Myers as the victim turned victimizer. Critics have sometimes described him as "a child in an adult's body who exerts a repressed rage . . . against sexually promiscuous females (representing his own sister)" and members of his own family. His initial killing of his older sister is related, inconclusively, to some undisclosed family trauma, perhaps to Michael's incestuous feelings for her.[22] Myers's own doctor, Sam Loomis (played by Donald Pleasance), very occasionally offers this kind of explanation, attempting in *Halloween 5* (1989) to reason with Myers about the psychotic rage that drives him to seek vengeance upon his family.

Yet Loomis consistently repudiates his own professional discourse by describing Myers as the very embodiment of evil, implacably impervious to therapeutic treatment. This interpretation trades on the popular fascination with the personification of evil touted by the evangelical Right and deepened by a skepticism of rehabilitative treatment in corrective or psychiatric institutions. Indeed, more often than not, Myers is depicted as a mythic, elusive bogeyman, one of superhuman strength who cannot be killed by bullets, stab wounds, or fire. In the first *Halloween*, Myers endures two stab wounds, and a round of bullets that propel him over a balcony, only to vanish into nowhere. In *Halloween 4*, he survives a car collision, a hail of bullets from the state troopers, and a headlong fall into a deep well. And he somehow manages to transmit the "evil" within him to his niece Jaimie Strode,

Michael Myers electrocutes a utility worker, from *Halloween 4*.

who at the finale of the film, kills her own stepmother with a knife in a scene that reenacts Myers's murder of his own sister when he was eight years old. Only in *Halloween H20* (1998) is this seemingly invincible bogeyman finally dispatched by his intrepid sister, Laurie, who has sought to escape the family curse by taking up residence in California. She decapitates Michael with an axe. Perhaps this will not be the last word on Michael Myers. Perhaps, like Frankenstein's monster, he will be crudely sutured together or genetically reconstituted, as was Ripley in *Alien Resurrection*, to haunt his family again.

Clearly, one can suspend belief on Myers if one so chooses and even render the whole Halloween cycle sociologically irrelevant. One of the first reviews of *Halloween* in the *Village Voice* veered in this direction, applauding the director, John Carpenter, for his clever intertextual play on other movies in the genre, particularly Hitchcock's *Psycho* and Romero's *Night of the Living Dead*. "Carpenter's duplicitous hype is the most honest way to make a good schlock film," remarked Tom Halen, making it "the trickiest thriller of the year."[23]

But not every critic has viewed the film so light-heartedly, especially in the light of its popularity. Modestly budgeted and promoted, *Halloween* earned $18.5 million in the domestic market alone and became something of a cult movie with the video fans.[24] It also spawned a subgenre of stalker movies that many noted was disturbingly sadistic and misogynist in its voyeurism. Critics Mick Martin and Marsha Porter, for instance, took great exception to the first-person camera shots of both *Halloween* and *Friday the 13th* (1980), films that encouraged an identification with the killer and sometimes depicted the graphic dismemberment of victims, especially females. They deplored the way in which "the camera moves in on the screaming, pleading victim, 'looks down' at the knife, and then plunges it into chest, ear, or eyeball. Now that's sick."[25]

How misogynist these films really are has generated a good deal of heated debate, particularly among feminist film critics. While some have seen the slasher movies since *Halloween* as debasing women in as decisive a manner as hard-core pornography, others have read the genre in a more positive light. While most have admitted that the camera lingers primarily on female victims, they have resisted the inclination to describe the films as unequivocally misogynistic. Writing from a postmodern perspective, film critic Carol Clover has noted that the subjective camera does not consistently adhere to the male assaultive gaze. The jerky visions of the camera do not simply signify the deranged passion of the killer, she argues, but hint also at the killer's eventual demise. Through the eye of the camera, the killer's gaze is unstable, destructive, and destructible.[26]

Moreover, the misogynist thrust of slasher movies is undermined by the fact that the "final girl" ultimately triumphs. This is in marked contrast to earlier horror films, where the menace was usually terminated by professionally motivated men. If women are the principal subjects of abject terror, rendered helpless before the killer's gaze, they also lay that gaze to rest. Whether this is a typical trait of post-1968 horror, however, is hotly contested, as is the gendered depiction of the victor, whose female persona might simply be a cover for masculine or more androgynous traits.

How these issues are played out in the Halloween movies is worth considering. Although the police rescue the "final girl" from the grips of the psychotic killer in *Hollowgate* (1988), in half of the Halloween movies the finale does depart from the older formula of a male protector putting the threat to rest. In the *Halloween* cycle, the police are generally portrayed as incompetent, as vulnerable as many of the besieged teenagers to the avenger's knife. So, too, are the professionals. In the first *Halloween* (1978), the psychiatrist Dr. Loomis puts Laurie and her friends at risk by misreading Myers's intentions and recommending that no general alarm be raised about the escape of the killer from the hospital. Only in the final scene does Loomis come to Laurie's aid in her desperate struggle with Myers. In the sequel, Loomis is more concerned about Laurie's safety and even helps her dispatch Myers by fire, scarring himself in the process. But thereafter Loomis's obsession

Jaimie cowering in fear of Michael Myers, from *Halloween 5*.

with tracking the killer becomes progressively ineffectual and even ruthlessly self-interested. By *Halloween 5*, he is holding Myers's niece, Jaimie, as live bait. "You want her?" he screams to Myers. "Here she is. Come and get her. Come and get your little girl."

The only male who effectually comes to the rescue of members of Myers's family is their friend Tommy Doyle. In *Halloween 6*, he saves Jaimie's baby from the hands of the satanic Dr. Wynn and the implacable Michael Myers. Elsewhere it is the women who elude and even take on the zombie-like Myers. In *Halloween 4*, this is left to Jaimie's stepsister, Rachel, who, having witnessed the death of her boyfriend at the hands of Myers, helps Jaimie escape over the roof to comparative safety and, in their flight out of town, mows down Myers with a pick-up truck. Her heroism, nonetheless, is short-lived. Like Alice in *Friday the 13th*, she falls victim to Myers in the sequel. In the end, it is only Michael's sister, Laurie, who is able to come to terms with the family monster. In *Halloween* she stabs Michael in the eye and the body before Loomis comes to the rescue. In the sequel she sinks into an abject terror that virtually paralyzes her. Only as a mature woman in the final film of the cycle does she take on Myers single-handedly. Overcoming her own nightmares about Michael's devastating rage, she ultimately stalks and slays her brother with an axe.

Whether there is enough in all this to vindicate the feminist reading of the "final girl" is debatable. In *Halloween H20*, Laurie's final victory over Myers could simply be read as a cinematic play on the Leigh family's contribution to horror over the years, juxtaposing Janet Leigh, the abject victim of *Psycho*, against her real-life daughter, Jamie Lee Curtis, the intrepid Laurie who eludes and finally kills Myers. Moreover, it has been argued that the independence and resolution of "final girls" such as Laurie is less emphatic or consistent than feminist critics assume. Some of them, like the sole survivor in *Hollowgate*, are rendered catatonic by the experience. In any case, it has been argued, their triumphs permit only a highly individualistic response to the perceived threat, not collective solutions.

For some critics, the issues surrounding the subjective camera and the voyeuristic gaze are less important than what the stalker movies reveal about family tensions in America. In the opinion of critic Tony Williams, the films of the 1980s spoke revealingly to the conservative family values of Reaganite America, with patriarchal avatars such as Myers punishing both sexual permissiveness and dysfunctional families, particularly families without strong fathers.[27] Although the depiction of Myers as victim turned victimizer might have invited a social critique of the problems besetting the American family, his demonization inhibited it. Far from representing the return of the repressed, Myers became a scapegoat for familial disorder.

This interpretation is intriguing. Whether we find the neo-Freudian analysis compelling or not, it has the great merit of setting the *Halloween* cycle within the larger contemporary debate about the future of the American family, one that in the 1970s was preoccupied with high divorce rates, the rise of double-income households, gender politics, and same-sex coupling. This debate, with its anxieties about working mothers, single-parent families, and unsupervised children, provided the social space in which Myers's sanguinary escapades could strike admonitory chords. For it could be argued that Myers's murderous interventions are facilitated by the collapse of Halloween as an inclusive family holiday and its transformation into a set of generational consumer rites in which family mutualities are neglected. While parents are partying (or working), teenagers raise mayhem or make out and neglect the youngsters in their care. In this allegory of familial dispersal and decay, where Halloween is viewed nostalgically as a potentially unifying and satisfying family rite, killers more easily prowl.

Yet the contemporary controversies surrounding the holiday itself would also seem to be relevant to the narrative of fear these movies seek to construct, at least as immediate referents. The Halloween films opened in the wake of the billowing stories about Halloween sadism and clearly traded on the uncertainties surrounding trick-or-treating and the general safety of the festival. In *Halloween 2*, a child is taken to the hospital after a razor has been found in his apple. In *Night of the Demons*, an angry householder threatens to taint the apples of a group of gallivanting teenagers and, in the final scene, falls victim to his own artifice. Here the urban legends about Halloween sadism are little more than embellishments to the main narrative, but in *Halloween 3*, the threat to children is central to the story. Conal Cochran is the ultimate Halloween sadist, the malevolent predator on the lives of innocent children, transforming their masks into deadly weapons of destruction.

Concurrent with the growing fear that Halloween was becoming a macabre festival of sadistic acts was the public fascination with serial killers. The term "serial killer" did not enter public discourse until the early 1980s, when the subject was widely aired on TV programs such as Chris Wilder's *Easy Prey* and the miniseries about Ted Bundy entitled *The Deliberate Stranger*. In fact, the Tylenol scare of 1982 was quickly followed by a public panic about serial killers, prompted by the fact that the U.S. Department of Justice had speculated that the phenomenon was on the rise. Without doubt, the supersession of the classic horror film monsters by omnipotent serial killers was not coincidental. Although neither Jason of the *Friday the 13th* series nor Michael Myers of the *Halloween* cycle conformed exactly to the prototypes of serial killers—people who often relished the power they had over their victims—their grisly escapades were intended to strike more than a frisson of fear in a public troubled by the potential terror of everyday life and the growing number of unresolved homicides. As the cultural critic Jonathan Crane observed, the new horror genre offered "a visual approximation of what it is like to live in an inordinately dangerous world of random violence."[28]

If the *Halloween* cycle traded on contemporary panics, it also depicted and helped to reinforce the hyperreality that increasingly distinguishes the holiday. "Hyperreality" is a term coined by Jean Baudrillard to depict a universe of signs in which the distinction between the real and imaginary is not simply blurred but eliminated. What is created is an order of simulations without external referents, a world of reality effects.

The current practice of Halloween, with its spook houses, terror trains, films, and videos consistently flirts with and teeters on the brink of this universe. Is Jason real or the product of cinematic representation? What does one make of his appearance on the Arsenio Hall show where he was treated like any other celebrity and asked what he had been doing lately?[29] (As Jonathan Crane has remarked, Jason makes no career moves, he just slashes people.) At what point, amid the holographic effects and screams in stereo, does the safe spook of the haunted house become a macabre act of violence? Halloween horror could be the real thing. At Greenfield, Massachusetts, in 1988, a fan of Jason was rumored to have carried out a copycat murder on Fright Night.[30] Although psychologists believe that even children of eight or nine can distinguish the real from the phoney, the effects of the blurring can be seen not only in the persistent legend of the Halloween sadist tainting children's candies and inserting razors into apples but in the haunting slayings of the slasher movies. In 1991, rumors of an impending massacre on Halloween, foretold by a psychic on the Oprah Winfrey show, generated anxieties throughout the sororities of Northeast campuses that university authorities found difficult to dispel.[31] Halloween has become captive to *horror vacui*, in Umberto Eco's words, to an imagination that "demands the real thing and, to attain it, must fabricate the absolute fake."[32]

The fascination with the fake and the marketability of fear at Halloween is underlined in the following story. In 1976, a teenager named Bill Schuck, who called himself the "Devil's Advocate," opened a spook house in Miramar, Florida. With its dismembered bodies, rain, thunder, and lightning, its life-like figures of Frankenstein's monster and Regan from the *Exorcist* (1973), it attracted hundreds of visitors. The Halloween spectacle was so successful it attracted the attention of the California Institute of the Arts, founded by Walt Disney, who asked for a portfolio of the enterprise.[33] The links were instructive, because in the 1970s Halloween increasingly drew on the horror genre for its scary thrills. Like Disneyland itself, it was becoming a "perfect model of all the entangled orders of simulation."[34]

The melding of Hollywood with Halloween and the critical importance of hyperrealism to modern mass culture can also be seen in ventures such as Spooky World, a horror theme park near Foxboro, Massachusetts. Here, for $23.50, visitors can enjoy not only haunted hayrides but also a ghoul school run by Tom Savani, the "godfather" of special effects for films such as *Night of the Living Dead*, *Friday the 13th*, and *Creepshow*. Among the other celebrities featured in the 2000 season were Doug Bradley, the "Pinhead" in *Hellraiser*; and Richard Kiel, the "Jaws" of two James Bond movies. The ghoulish rock star Alice Cooper also joined this grisly crew, as did several WWF wrestlers and Brinke Stevens of *Swamp Thing* (1982), profiled on the Internet in S&M leather gear. However you take your Halloween, whatever fantasies you wrap around it, Spooky World is likely to have them in its seasonal simulations.

⚜ 6 ⚜
Stepping Out

In 1983, a Washington journalist described the Halloween street parade at Georgetown, albeit in a campy style and with a profusion of mixed metaphors. "At Wisconsin and M," he wrote,

> in the belly of the blast, it was like an Easter parade of freaks . . . to say nothing of the flashers who offered outrageous peaks. As Washington staked its claim as San Francisco East, glitter and gloss were everywhere and the roar of the grease-paint and the swell of the crowd engulfed Georgetown, magically transpoofing it into an androgynous and anthropomorphic street fair. Men dressed as women; women dressed as men; . . . men and women dressed as things that could heal the sick, raise the dead and make little girls talk out of their heads. Acting out their most sublimated fantasies, strutting their stuff, whirring and purring like figurines on an elaborate cuckoo clock. As Butch said to Sundance, "Who *are* those guys?"[1]

"Those guys" were part of the crowds who participated in annual street carnivals that punctuated the decade. From Halifax to Vancouver,

Dressed for the party, Toronto, 1995. *Photo by Nick Rogers.*

from New York City to Los Angeles, revelers congregated in downtown cores to commemorate All Hallow's Eve in tens and sometimes hundreds of thousands. Halloween went big-time in the 1970s and 1980s, eclipsing the child-centered rituals of trick-or-treating with what another journalist described as "escapist extravaganzas" that "more resembled Mardi Gras than the candy-and-apple surfeits of yesteryear."[2] In San Francisco, alongside huge gay promenades at Castro and Polk Streets, the Trocadero Transfer Club ran a three-day bash on the theme of the Australian cult movie, *The Road Warrior*.[3] At Salem, Massachusetts, witchery generated forty events for some 50,000 visitors. Even in Salt Lake City, where the Mormons frowned on public profanity and excess, private clubs promoted Halloween parties with gusto. One observer remembered pregnant nuns and lewd priests cavorting on the dance floor, and three gold-painted angels mimicking the figure atop the city's Mormon temple.[4] Amid the voyeurism and exhibitionism, the carnivalesque seemed irrepressible.

Street parades and dances were, of course, hardly new to Halloween. In mid-nineteenth-century Philadelphia, where festive mummery had strong roots, young men would dress in fancy costumes and congregate at bars and taverns.[5] In Montreal, young guisers often marched up and down rue St. Denis before turning off to visit friends and neighbors. By the 1920s, the Montreal West municipality had taken charge of these festivities by organizing a formal parade for the young children, one which gave way to more adult activities as the night wore on, including street dancing, masquerading, cabarets, and drinking.[6]

So there was nothing particularly novel about stepping out on Halloween, least of all for adults. Halloween parades, dances, and cabarets were all part of the festive fun in the 1920s, although their tone and temper would vary from place to place, depending upon the

Tinsel Man, Toronto, 1999.
Photo by Nick Rogers.

Dancing to the beat,
Halloween as adult party.
Photo by Nick Rogers.

visibility of church organizations and both official and public attitudes toward temperance. What was noteworthy was the efflorescence of the street promenade in the more permissive climate of the 1970s, after years of decline. In this decade Halloween reached beyond the traditional church hall and community fair to encompass the bar, night club, disco, and street. This expansion of public space was encouraged by an entertainment industry that sought to profit from a licensed moment of conspicuous consumption, whether that meant cruising bars or parading around in rented costumes.[7]

Yet the new-style Halloween also represented a public demand for cathartic release. As one journalist remarked of the Georgetown promenade in Washington: "In a city where work is the chief narcotic, fun is the prescribed antidote." Or as a librarian at the Folger put it: "You have to follow rules in everyday [life], but on Halloween you can dress up according to your fantasy."[8] Those fantasies were still drawn from the modern motifs of Halloween, with witches, werewolves, ghosts, and vampires in abundance. But they were increasingly derived from television and Hollywood, with ugly beasts from *Return of the Jedi* and Jason look-a-likes cutting through the crowds with chainless chainsaws.[9]

If much of the dressing-up on Halloween was simply exhibitionist or the sublimation of some personal fantasy, it also evoked social comment. The early Greenwich Village parades, for example, featured mythic old women or "hags" on stilts, who symbolically reclaimed the streets from the automobile on behalf of local communities. Many of the participants in the parade also celebrated the grotesque, parodying the sleek, photogenic models of the fashion magazines with ungainly, protuberant bodies redolent of early modern European carnivals, where the grotesque was often contrasted to the statuesque.[10] In a gruesome scenario that touched the raw nerves of contemporary debate, a woman in a white wedding dress was depicted aborting a fully formed fetus into a cardboard package labeled "Human Organ for Transplant. Handle with Care." A werewolf dressed in black sprinkled pepper on the "transplant," compounding bad taste with a hint of cannibalism.[11]

Not all costumes were so sanguinary. Sometimes they parodied mass culture à la Andy Warhol: a gasoline pump, a vending machine, a trash can, a tube of Crest toothpaste, a tube of lipstick, a piece of masticated chewing-gum, a corn flake, a six-pack of beer, a hot dog, a couch potato.[12] In New York in the early 1990s, two gay men dressed as cocktails, a pun on their sexuality as well as parody of consumer culture. In Toronto in 1998, one woman dressed as a carton of McDonald's fries, with McDyke as the logo, a play on the straight, all-American orientation of the infamous fast-food chain.[13]

Other masqueraders echoed the sick jokes of Lenny Bruce: replicating Tylenol bottles at the height of the contamination scare in 1982, for example; or dressing as herpes lesions while dancing to the tune of "Strangers in the Night."[14] Still others took Halloween as an occasion to parody the consumer ethic by handing out fake money to passers-by. "Here's $10,000," declared one Georgetown money-tree, "that ought to hold you till tomorrow."[15] Halloween could thus become a satire on the vacuity and banality of consumer society, on the production of false needs, even if the holiday itself was saturated with consumerism.

Masquerading also gives revelers the chance to spoof celebrities or politicians. In 1994, for example, the public's fascination with the O. J. Simpson trial prompted the appearance of a number of O. J. costumes on Halloween, complete with Afro wig, football jersey, and bloody glove; "a fashionable ghoulishness," remarked the *Christian Science Monitor*, "with a touch of racism thrown in." Because Halloween also happens to coincide with the U.S. presidential campaign every four years, the candidates inevitably capture the limelight. In 1988, one Washington bar invited revelers to turn out as their favorite, George Bush look-a-likes outnumbering those of Michael Dukakis by 108 to 86.[16] Ten years later, Bill Clinton's sexual peccadilloes were mocked in the shape of Monica Lewinskys. Parodying the Pope, of course, is always fair game. The Washington street parade of 1980 featured one Pope John Paul II cavorting with a Playboy bunny. It also had Richard Nixon and Ronald Reagan look-a-likes kissing one another in a like-minded embrace. "Nuke Iran, nuke welfare, nuke the babies!" cried the latter.

Parodying American presidents has become something of a tradition on Halloween, but Canadian politicians have seldom escaped a roasting, either. In 1987, a Brian Mulroney look-a-like entertained spectators in Halifax only days after the Prime Minister had been hissed and booed by unemployed steelworkers from his former riding of Central Nova Scotia.[17]

Yet beyond the personalities of the hour, the holiday has also given revelers a chance to promote a range of causes, whether national or local. In the wake of the terrorist attack on the World Trade Center in September 2001, there was a genuine desire in the Unitied States to show the flag on Halloween. Costume firms were quick to notice this and promote it. One firm urged consumers to "show your patriotism" by purchasing outfits of Miss Liberty, astronauts, commandos, policemen, firefighters, construction workers, Texan cowboys, and, of course, Uncle Sam. His full costume was priced at $160, and a more deluxe, sequined version at $375.[18]

Since the 1970s the political causes promoted at Halloween have been diverse. In the past, revelers have masqueraded as the "Red Menace," with a hammer and sickle painted on their faces, or joined a swarm of phantom cyclists to take back the streets from the omnipresent automobile, as happened recently in Toronto. In 1975, a group of masked protesters, calling themselves the Phantom tax squad, campaigned outside the offices of Duquesne Light on Sixth Avenue in Pittsburgh, claiming that the public utility company had misappropriated the federal taxes that it had collected from the public.[19] More flamboyantly, Greenwich Village parade artists have satirized the inconveniences of modern urban living by creating huge models of giant roach motels and malfunctioning subway cars. In 1987, the year of the Wall Street mini-crash, one guiser portrayed Death as a Chicago future. Another, more ecologically conscious, depicted the fate of Californian grape-growers laboring under hazardous pesticides in the shape of the Grim Reaper.[20] A few years later, three drag queens dressed as Brazilian *caricata*—mock-females with exaggerated buttocks and bosoms—parodied the Desert Storm campaign, embellishing their outfits with plastic tanks, rifles, knives, binoculars, hand-grenade earrings, and green helmets with Storm veterans' patches on the front.[21]

The political dimensions of Halloween are important in one other respect, one that bears directly on the identity politics of postmodern culture. Feminists have from time to time tailored Halloween to their needs. In 1968, when feminists were disrupting beauty pageants and bridal fairs, the Women's International Terrorist Conspiracy from Hell (WITCH) descended upon Wall Street, demanding an end to the "death-dealing sexual, economic and spiritual repression of the Imperialist Phallic Society" and advocating full equality for men and women within a "truly cooperative" world.[22] Two years later, "sister witches" in Ann Arbor paraded through the streets banging pots and pans, "haunting and hexing" nine symbols of male dominance, including the residence of the university president and a pornography store. Along the way they chanted "male chauvinists better start shaking, today's pig is tomorrow's bacon."[23] The following year, a group of a women calling themselves the "No More Tricks or Treats Committee" marched on the 59th Street Playboy Club in New York City to protest the absence of male bunnies and the "uncomfortable restrictive bunny suits" of the females.[24] More recently, feminists have appropriated the witch motif of Halloween to emphasize women's inner wisdom and spirituality in a bellicose, macho society.[25]

Yet it has been the gay community that has most flamboyantly exploited Halloween's potential as a transgressive festival, as one that operates outside or on the margins of orthodox time, space, and hierarchy.[26] Indeed, it is the gay community that has been arguably most responsible for Halloween's adult rejuvenation. Transvestism has long been part of Halloween, albeit as a temporary transference of gender identity. "Hallowe'en is the one evening of the year when Jacques can masquerade as Jacqueline and Jacqueline as Jacques," remarked the *Montreal Gazette* in 1931.[27] Not everyone responded to cross-dressing with such equanimity. In Toronto at the turn of the twentieth century, a sixteen-year-old lad named William Lee "thought to honour the occasion by arraying himself in a girl's skirt and bodice," a "meta-morphosis," the *Mail* remarked, that drew comments "more pointed than polite."[28] Even so, cross-dressing remained a constituent feature of Halloween, harking back to the boy-choristers of early modern Hallowmass.

Philadelphia appears to have been one of the first American cities to stage drag parades on Halloween. Transvestism had conventionally been part of the Mummers' Parade in the city, and it was not surprising that it spilled over to Halloween.[29] In the 1940s and 1950s, hundreds of drag queens paraded along Locust Street, moving in and out of the local bars, and within a few years African-American gays began to stage their own parade on South Street, moving in and out of Pep's, Nick's, and Showboat. These Halloween promenades became so well known that

Drag queens, Toronto,
1998. *Photo by Nick Rogers.*

thousands traveled to Philadelphia to cheer, yell, and gawk at the gays, usually in a nonconfrontational way. One cross-dresser recalled that he "didn't see anything but good nature, unless they were tourists who were just there with their mouths open to their shoes and not saying anything, just in total disbelief."[30] One black drag queen, however, remembered having her clothes ripped off on the Broad Street promenade. Indeed, by 1962, the homophobic violence had reached such proportions that the police decided to shut down the parades. This did not inhibit cross-dressing. According to one Philadelphian, gay Halloween continued to be "a real event, every bit as exciting as Halloween is in West Hollywood or in New Orleans. . . . People would dress up or not, do outrageous impromptu parades in cars and convertibles. People would ride around on the hoods of cars and walk down the streets kissing strangers."[31]

As gay parades disappeared from Philadelphia, so they began to spring up elsewhere, wherever the gay community felt confident enough to celebrate their sexuality and affirm their right to public space. In 1971, for example, gays in San Francisco traveled around the city on buses on Halloween,

> the famous and glamorous queen leading her entourage from bar to bar, showing off her following and the creations she inspired for them. Bus after bus pulled up to the bars and the Sixth Street auditorium of the Society for Individual Rights [a gay organization]. There were, at SIR, a panel of judges rating the drag queens on the dresses they wore, their poise, and how well they carried off the intended illusion.[32]

In the same year in New York City, a Broadway drag rock show from San Francisco, starring the Cockettes—"a spangled chaos of flesh, a seething mass of hock-shop costumes, doing their thing for freedom"— staged an impromptu Halloween parade on East 9th Street.[33] Within a few years, gay promenades had become a constituent feature of the Greenwich Village Halloween celebrations. Beginning in 1974 as a countercultural event for the Village arts community, this annual parade, with its puppets, floats, and revelers, has become a fixture in Gotham's calendar. By the mid-1980s, it was attracting thousands of participants as well as hundreds of thousands of spectators. As an unofficial adjunct to the main procession, New York gays staged their own drag parade, strutting their stuff on Christopher Street.[34]

Gay parades in cities like New York and San Francisco featured all manner of sexual parodies. In 1979, the Castro Street parade in San Francisco featured several super-macho hard hats, a Miss Piggy, an eighteenth-century courtesan, a bevy of moustached, muscular cheerleaders of the Oakland Raiders, and a number of Jackie Kennedys in bloodstained pink dresses. In this way they poked fun at mainstream definitions of "male" and "female," including the female icon of Camelot, America's most charismatic first lady. Vulgar feminist perceptions of gender politics were also mocked. In 1987, a Greenwich Village group of transvestites accompanied a man dressed in a long brown costume with several sheets of toilet paper affixed to it. "We're out with our date," one of the queens remarked: "He's dressed as a turd because everyone knows that all men are shits."[35]

Amid the exhibitionism it is worth stressing that drag was always *the* motif of the gay parade. Embodying the negative stereotype of the homosexual male in mainstream culture, drag was redefined by gays as something positive and desirable and as a satire on hetero-stereotypes of "real," sexually desirable women.[36] The double entendres made for some heady body politics, both within and outside the gay community. Some gays saw Halloween as "a small but significant skirmish in the wars of sexual liberation." Others feared that this annual "drag night" would irreparably ghettoize and stigmatize the homosexual and generate an orgy of gay bashing.[37] In fact, in Toronto, where gay parades on Halloween had been held since the early 1970s, political pressure had to be put on the police to assist gay volunteers in controlling the hostile crowds who gathered to jeer the drag parade at Wellesley and Yonge Streets.[38] Public space for gays, whether in Toronto or elsewhere, was not lightly won.

In the wake of the gay street promenades, more and more hetero-sexuals took to the street. In Washington's Georgetown, the number of promenaders at Wisconsin and M swelled to 150,000 at its prime; Hollywood's annual Halloween blast reached similar numbers. In Halifax, Nova Scotia, where local businessmen first promoted a Halloween masquerade in a downtown tavern in 1981, the event became so popular that the city decided to cordon off an area around Argyle Street to accommodate the crowds. By the end of the decade, as many as 40 to 50,000 people congregated to watch this "Mardi Gras," as it was called. Even in Toronto, where the police allowed automobiles to venture down Yonge Street, crowds of 50,000 blocked the sidewalks to gawk at the revelers, drop into the bars, and generally to enjoy the hilarity of the night.

Big-city street parties sometimes have a limited time span. Washington's revel at Wisconsin and M was crippled by the prohibitive cost of policing the event, some $284,000 in extra pay in 1990, and also by fears of physical danger, especially in the wake of a fatal stabbing in a Georgetown bar in 1989. From a peak of 150,000 celebrants in 1987, the Georgetown revel had declined to 30,000 by 1990, and was so quiet that year that one resident thought the Halloween gathering had been canceled.[39] Halifax's Mardi Gras also shows signs of waning in popularity, as arrests for drunkenness increase and the clean-up bill to the city reaches $10,000.[40]

As this evidence suggests, Halloween can certainly have its degenerative side. The promoters of Canada's East Coast revel forgot that Mardi Gras required some sort of infrastructure beyond organizing an indoor costume competition. New Orleans has always had its krewes and Rio de Janeiro its samba clubs. New York's Greenwich Village parade has always had a committee that raises funds and works with the Village's artistic community in promoting particular themes each Halloween. Although anyone can join the parade, these advance preparations ensure a modicum of continuity from year to year. Without this organizational structure, the success of Halloween parades and promenades is left largely to chance. In Halifax, the civic authorities were reluctant to intervene in the celebrations on the grounds that this would ruin their spontaneity. But ultimately they found themselves allying with the police to prevent the Mardi Gras from becoming little more than a hellish bender, by banning alcohol, for instance, on the streets in 1990.

Yet walking the wild side on Halloween will likely persist. As journalist Ellen Creager noted in 1990, Halloween is "free-form, homemade, the most rebellious of holidays and the one with the fewest expectations. It's the only holiday that refuses to take itself seriously."[41]

For students, yuppies, and for young people in general, that is part of its appeal. It has an infectious, playful quality that is difficult to dispel. Halloween is a mind-bender. It is an opportunity to act out one's desires or fantasies without social or—within limits—official recrimination.

In this respect, Halloween is not unlike Mardi Gras, the festival that celebrates the exuberance of life and the pleasures of the body and parodies, while anticipating, the constraints and discipline of the coming Lent. Like Mardi Gras, Halloween emphasizes appetite, desire, and feeling rather than duty, obligation, or formal allegiance. It does so as a form of "framed play," to use a concept of Victor Turner,[42] within sites and times that are bordered or bounded. People act out on Halloween in ways that they do not normally do.

Halloween is unquestionably a night of inversion. But is it subversive rather than simply transgressive? Does it challenge preconceived notions of how society operates in a determined or sustained way? At a profound level, probably not. At its best, Halloween functions as a transient form of social commentary or "deep play." From time to time it has been an important site of identity politics. It has been used to promote certain causes and to broaden social consciousness, particularly at the Greenwich Village parade. Here the public liminality of the night, the holiday's capacity to transcend everyday social constraints, to think of possibilities rather than actualities, intersects with the artistic avant-garde.[43] As even the *National Review* admitted, the political temper of the parades, in the early years at least, tended to be left of center, a counterpoint to the New York of the stockbroker and international financier.[44]

Yet much of the social criticism expressed on Halloween tends to be transitory and ephemeral. Halloween has never been a time of sustained social and political debate, as was the Fourth of July in the early years of the American republic.[45] Its signifying practices tend to be decentered, dispersed, and centripetal, forever moving outward. Humor and play, the dominant tropes of Halloween, can best parody power rather than subvert it.

The cultural inversion of Halloween, the temporary slackening or reversal of norms, can in fact move in deadly, antisocial directions. In the last decade, adolescent anti-Semitism on Halloween led to the desecration of a local synagogue in Clifton, New Jersey, and attacks upon the homes and businesses of leading members of the Jewish community.[46] There have also been a series of "wilding" sprees on Halloween in which women have been raped and stabbed and the homeless bludgeoned. In 1990, a Boston gang called the Pistons raped and brutally murdered a twenty-six-year-old single mother on a Halloween "wilding spree."[47] The poor woman was found naked in Franklin Field with over 130 stab wounds to her body. The same year, a gang of youths from the East River projects in Manhattan, some sporting Halloween masks, descended upon the homeless of Ward's Island with bats, pipes, cleavers, and knives; taunted them with cries of "trick or treat"; wounded several; and left one for dead among the garbage-strewn weeds. According to press reports, the rampage was the culmination of a series of attacks against the homeless, whose drug abuse and pilfering had angered local residents and provided a pretext for recriminatory violence. "It happens a lot here, every Halloween," scoffed one youth, who seemed to resent the media attention the incident had received. "I don't see what the big deal is."[48]

The attack upon the homeless of New York's East Side in 1990 followed a time-honored script, with masked redressers taking advantage of the festive license customarily accorded youth on Halloween to eliminate elements that they perceived as harmful to their community. The incident forcibly reminds us, in the words of Le Roy Ladurie, that "popular festivities and social change do not always go hand in hand."[49] If Halloween can provide a space for cultural diversity and pluralism, it can also prompt community intolerance of the marginal. Like carnivals, Halloween "can constitute a symbolic rebellion by the weak or a festive scapegoating of the weak, or both at the same time."[50]

☾ 7 ☾

BORDER CROSSINGS

As I suggested in the preceding chapter, Halloween was revitalized in the 1970s as a holiday of youthful license and difference. It continued to retain some of the spirit of premodern festivals, whose topsy-turvy rituals and liminal spaces afforded some opportunity to parody mainstream culture, to blow off steam, and to express alternative sexualities and ways of seeing the world. Yet since the 1920s, Halloween has also been seen as a homogenizing force or, at the very least, a marker of the cultural mainstream. French-Canadians living in Quebec City did not celebrate Halloween until the 1960s.[1] Only those living in Montreal, or on the borders of Ontario, would have come into contact with and arguably participated in what must have seemed an "Anglo" holiday. And if French-Canadians found Halloween too Anglo a holiday, Jews found its Christian overtones off-putting. As my Jewish dentist confided in me, he celebrated Halloween in the 1950s in spite of his parents, raiding the corner store with kids from the neighborhood and inflicting pranks on storekeepers who had covered their apples with hot pepper.

For many immigrants to North America, moreover, Halloween must seem uniquely American or Canadian, an integral part of North American mass culture. Because shops are full of Halloween motifs from mid-September onward, because Halloween costume parties have become integral to school calendars, families with children cannot easily avoid the holiday. Consequently, immigrant families from places where Halloween is unknown are necessarily confronted with the problem of whether or when they should introduce their children to the rituals of trick-or-treat and seasonal masking, and on what terms. One of my associates at York University, who hails from Guyana, cautiously introduced her three-year-old son to the festival by buying candies for the local children who would come knocking at her door. She thought it important that her son should have some knowledge of the holiday before he entered school.

The question of how people from diverse cultural backgrounds might handle Halloween is dramatically posed in the American Southwest, where two different ways of celebrating 31 October and the days that follow confront one another, namely, Halloween and its Mexican counterpart, the Day of the Dead. *El Dia de los Muertos*, to use but one of the Spanish terms for the holiday, is a significant festival among Mexicans. It is a time for commemorating the dead and for con-solidating familial memories about those who have passed on. Its juxtaposition to Halloween is important because Mexicans are the largest group of immigrants entering the United States at the current time. They constitute a significant proportion of the Hispanic population that has doubled in the last twenty years or so, from 4.6 percent of the U.S. population in 1970 to 9.2 percent in 1990.[2] Densely clustered in specific states and cities, with birth rates higher than those of Anglos or blacks, they are an important presence in America's new cultural mosaic. Demographic projections suggest they will make the United States the third largest Spanish-speaking nation in the world within twenty years.

In Texan cities such as San Antonio, there has been an exuberant revival of the Day of the Dead as a symbol of Chicano cultural pride.[3] Alongside the actual recuperation of the holiday, which according to some contemporary observers was in danger of being lost in the melting pot of Americanization, there has been an active fusion of Halloween and the Day of the Dead among Anglo and Mexicano artists, and a blending of the two traditions at a more popular level. Pumpkins sometimes adorn the gravesites and *ofrendas* (family altars) in the San Fernando cemetery of San Antonio. Papier-mâché witches sit beside the skeletons and *calaveras* (skulls) that typify the Day of the Dead celebrations. And Halloween treats now form part of the festive fare alongside the *pan de muertos,* the "bread of the dead" that is integral to the Mexican holiday.[4] According to the Institute of Texan Cultures, the last two decades have seen the creation of a uniquely Texan Day of the Dead that both incorporates elements of Halloween and affirms the new mood of multiculturalism in modern America.

The conjunction and potential fusion of the two holidays south of the Rio Grande, has been controversial, however, especially since the signing of the North American Free Trade Agreement (NAFTA), and the increasing penetration of American culture into Mexico. While many children in Mexico City have taken to the American holiday, stomping through the streets with their *calaveras* shouting "Dame Halloween," others have viewed Halloween as a corrosively commercial and culturally alien festival, disrupting the time-honored celebration of the Day of the Dead. Dr. Gonzalez-Crussi, for example, a professor of pathology and contributor to the *New Yorker,* found the emulation of Halloween in Mexico City to be disquieting. "Have we come this far," he asked his fellow Mexicans, "to see an imitation in third-world gear, of the North American Halloween?"[5] One nursery teacher from Puebla regarded Halloween as nothing less than an "invasion, as something that doesn't belong to us. Halloween is truly frightening for children, because it focuses on witches and witchcraft, sorcerers and devils. It deforms the imagination and threatens our indigenous traditions." To the local artists and confectioners who help make the Day of the Dead a colorful but respectful holiday in the Mexican calendar, the intrusion of Halloween motifs is distasteful and threatening. Novelist Homero Aridjis has even described Halloween as a form of "cultural pollution."[6]

Similar sentiments have been expressed in San Luis Potosi, where public schools have launched a "Say no to Halloween" campaign, deriding the holiday as "an assault similar to other depravities we've received from the North, like drug use."[7] These reactions refer principally to the more commercial variants of Halloween that penetrate the shops of Mexico's major cities, although behind the protests lie larger anxieties about how Mexico might modernize under NAFTA while retaining its own identity. In the case of Halloween, a festival that coincides with an officially sponsored national fiesta such as Dias de Muertos [31 October–2 November], the cultural exchanges are necessarily highly charged. And they are doubtless reinforced by the fact that many Halloween products are made by Hallmark, an American company that contracts some of its work to the *maquiladoras* along Mexico's border.[8] In this context, Halloween could represent the economic muscle of the United States as much as its cultural imperialism.

Yet however compelling and distasteful these Halloween signifiers are to Mexicans, they ignore the cultural politics that surround the event within North America and the manner in which Halloween has been creatively refashioned from the fragments, the *bricolage* of mass culture. Indeed, they invite us to compare the origins of Halloween and the Day of the Dead and the manner in which they have developed in very different cultural contexts.

Halloween and the Day of the Dead share a common origin in the Christian commemoration of the dead on All Saints' and All Souls' Day. But both are thought to embody strong pre-Christian beliefs. In the case of Halloween, the Celtic celebration of Samhain is critical to its pagan legacy, a claim that has been foregrounded in recent years by both new-age enthusiasts and the evangelical Right. In the case of the Day of the Dead, commentators routinely emphasize its pre-Columbian origins in the cults of the dead that abounded among the Nahuatl-speaking peoples of central Mexico. The anthropologist Hugo Nutini has identified seven annual occasions during which Mesoamericans worshipped, celebrated, or made sacrifices to the dead, underscoring the importance of the dead as intermediaries between humans and the gods. He has also noted those occasions, such as during the festivities of *Tepeilhuital*, when images of the dead were placed on family altars and food was offered to them, much in the manner of the *ofrendas* so central to the Day of the Dead.[9] Other authors have stressed the peculiarly culinary aspects of the Aztec mortuary ritual in which wooden images of the god Huitzilopochtli, the solar deity who emerged every morning from the earth goddess Coatlicue, were covered with a dough made of amaranth seed that was subsequently eaten by the celebrants. Early Spanish observers, in particular, remarked on the fabrication of idols from edible grains and their distribution as talismans or articles of communion.[10] They also noted the skulls of sacrificial victims that were publicly exhibited in rows (*tzompantli*) at the Toltec capital of Tula and at the Aztec capital of Tenochtitlan.[11] "The Mexicans being so very exact in all Religious Observances beyond all others in that new World," remarked the seventeenth-century Spanish historian Antonio de Herrera,

> either to shew the Multitude of Sacrifices they offer'd to their Gods, or to keep in their Minds the Remembrance of Death, to which all Men are subject, they had a Charnel of the Skulls of Men taken in War, and sacrific'd, which was without the Temple, and opposite to the great Gate . . . in Shape like a Theatre, longer than it was broad, strong, and built with Lime and Stone, with Steps, on which the Heads were set between the Stones, the Teeth outwards. At the Head and Foot of the Theatre were two Towers, made only of Lime and Skulls, and having no Stone or other Material, at least not to be seen; they were very strange to behold, being dreadful, and at the same Time a good Memorial, Death appearing which Way soever a Man turn'd his Eyes.[12]

This literary evidence, supported by archeological findings, is often taken as strong evidence that pre-Columbian practices were simply annexed to the festival of All Souls'; sometimes with the connivance of Franciscan friars who wished to encourage the rapid conversion of the indigenous population to Christianity and to soften the coercive character of their mission. Not all friars were so obliging, of course. Writing in 1580, Father Diego de Duran was troubled by the way in which indigenous cults of the dead were transposed to All Saints' and All Souls'. He was particularly concerned that All Saints' had become a festival devoted to little children who had died, thereby emulating the pre-Christian feast of Miccailhuitontli and Hueymiccaylhuitl, which had traditionally taken place two months earlier.[13]

Mexican scholars disagree over the influence of these ancient festivals upon the popular practice of Todos Santos (All Saints' and All Souls' Day), as the Day of the Dead is sometimes called. But an overemphasis on the continuities with the pre-Columbian past can easily elide the fact that there are also striking similarities between the rituals of the Day of the Dead and the early modern observance of All Souls' in Europe. Yellow flowers of mourning were common to both sixteenth-century Spain and Mexico. Ossuaries of skulls were part of the medieval rites of the dead, as were the animated skeletons of the *danses macabres* that graphically represented the ubiquity and inevitability of death. In the old Castilian province of Zamora, moreover, *ofrendas* and banquets were a customary aspect of funeral rites. In Barcelona, food stands routinely sold seasonal sweets called *panellets dels morts* on All Saints' Day. A variety of other cakes and sweets also formed part of the festive fare in Catalonia, Sardinia, Portugal, the Azores, and Haute-Saône in France, just as soul cakes were widely distributed in pre-Reformation Britain. What seems unique to the Mexican Todos Santos, and in fact to other parts of Spanish America such as Bolivia, was the widespread consumption of anthropomorphic foods, or foods in the shape of humans. These included the sugared skulls and figurines that now attract international attention, and the *pan de muertos*, "bread figures in the style of angels and human beings," which took on "a ritual character which is very important for all villagers."[14] These kinds of foods—breads

Time's Up. Death as the jester brings the final summons in a medieval *danse macabre*, from Hans Holbein's *Dance of Death*, 1538.

in human or animal form, in particular—were also made throughout the Iberian peninsula, though rarely for this holiday.[15]

There are grounds, then, for suggesting that the Mexican Day of the Dead was a complex mix of Mesoamerican and European influences, rather than a holiday onto which Christian observances were superficially superimposed. In this respect, the Day of the Dead was not so very different from Halloween. Both shared a common European legacy as well as a dynamic fusion of pre-Christian and Christian belief. If this is the case, then their differences may be grounded not only in the peculiarities of that syncretism, but also in the ways in which the two holidays subsequently developed in the New World. This aspect of the story is worth exploring further.

By the time Halloween was transposed to North America, its links to the Catholic festival of All Souls' were attenuated, seriously fractured by the Protestant Reformation. In some parts of Catholic Ireland, as we have seen, Halloween continued to be associated with All Souls' and the commemoration of the recently departed. Indeed, in some nineteenth-century Irish villages people still put out food for the returning spirits, in much the same way as did Mexicans, albeit without the elaborate *ofrendas* that graced their households. But this practice of putting out food for dead kin was a minority tradition that did not survive the transatlantic crossing.

Halloween in North America was a superstitious but increasingly secular holiday. It was largely divorced from the church services and graveside vigils of the faithful on All Souls'. These were customarily celebrated only by Catholics, and then as a holiday quite distinct from the Halloween revel. High birth rates and a growing expectation of life made the early American Halloween largely a matter of fireside hopes for good marriages than reflections on death, or the return of the dead. A mid-nineteenth-century New York edition of Burns's poems understood this quite clearly. The illustration accompanying the poem on Halloween portrayed a young man playfully grabbing a woman.[16]

The emphasis on life rather than death was also evident in the

Halloween customs of divining the future. In Newbell Puckett's Ohio collection of popular beliefs and superstitions, for example, Halloween divinations are principally associated with marriage, love, and the chances of becoming wealthy.[17] In only a few instances does the subject of death intrude upon the holiday, and then in rather Gothic contexts. One informant, for example, an African-American woman from Cleveland, believed that one should avoid cemeteries on Halloween because of the dangers of encountering life-destructive spirits. Another, an American female of Polish-Jewish extraction, thought that the disappearance of a stone from an outdoor fireplace on Halloween presaged one's death before the end of the year.

Predictably, the popular beliefs recorded in Puckett's collection betrayed a lingering sense of Halloween as a time of supernatural intensity. Ghosts emerged from the graves on Halloween, and souls or banshees roamed around to haunt wrong-doers. Replicating the rituals of All Souls', a few informants thought it important to leave food for the dead on tombstones or, in the Irish tradition, to put out boxey or boxty (fried colcannon) to appease the wandering souls who might be troublesome. Those troublesome souls also formed part of the folklore of Virginia and Maryland, and more generally the East Coast. Jack-o'-lanterns could lead children astray, spook farmers, and ensnare people "in the worst briers and brambles they could find." They were "little people," claimed one old woman in New York City, "misshapen and brown-skinned who carried small lanterns with them at night while hunting." The only way to thwart them was to lie down or turn one's coat inside out.[18]

By the mid-twentieth century, these folkloric tales were becoming increasingly marginal to mainstream belief, those concerning death in particular. Death had little dominion in North American Halloween, even though mortality rates ran at 35 to 39 per 1000 in cities such as Montreal during the 1870s, and one in four children died before the age of one until the end of the century.[19] By then, and certainly in the next two decades as infant mortality declined significantly, commemorating the dead on Halloween was very much a minority tradition. When death did return to Halloween, it was largely in the shape of Dracula, Frankenstein's monster, and later the lumbering figure of the serial killer Michael Myers. In other words, it was largely a product of the silver screen, often a reworking of the Gothic fascination with violence, eroticism, and the poltergeists of the imagination, themes that were the staple fare of nineteenth-century writers such as Robert Louis Stevenson and Edgar Allan Poe. Death as part of the cycle of life was not something that Halloween chose to commemorate. It confronted it only as a by-product of the uncanny and the repressed.

In Mexico, by contrast, the remembrance of the dead remained absolutely critical to Todos Santos. It was sustained by demographic catastrophe and the searing memory of colonial conquest. The coming of Hernando Cortez and his conquistadors brought military atrocity, harsh tributes, and epidemiological disaster to Mexico. Between 1519 and 1605, the population of central Mexico plummeted from 25 million people to just over a million. This astounding calamity was remembered in a ritualistically elaborate Day of the Dead that crystallized around 1610 in its early modern form. It was one that quickly assumed a central place in the Mexican calendar, rivaling Holy Week and the Day of the Virgin of Guadaloupe (12 December). Such memories of demographic devastation were reinforced by periodic crises of subsistence—ten in the years 1720–1810, one of which took over 300,000 lives[20]—and by high levels of infant mortality that persisted well into the twentieth century. As late as 1979, infant mortality stood at 62 per 1000 live births and at 90 per 1000 live births in poorer rural areas. Two decades earlier, it had been even worse. Although accurate figures are hard to come by, it has been claimed that in rural Tlaxcala, for example, half of all children died before the age of five, a rate of mortality that resembled seventeenth-century France, where, as Pierre Goubert has remarked, it took two children to make one adult.[21]

In the light of this demographic and colonial history, it is not difficult to understand the centrality of death in Mexican culture. "In Mexico," observed film-maker Sergei Eisenstein, "the paths of life and death intersect in a visual way, as they do nowhere else; this meeting is inherent both in the tragic image of death trampling on life, and with the sumptuous image of life triumphing over death."[22] This duality is present in the rituals surrounding the Day of the Dead. At their core are the commemorations at which families remember their own kin who have departed this world, from the preparation of *ofrendas*, where food and drink are left for the returning souls, to the vigils at the gravesides, which are cleaned up and decorated with flowers, candles, refurbished crosses, and sometimes photographs of the dead. These celebrations take place over several days, normally beginning on the afternoon of 31 October, when the souls of infants and children are thought to return. This day, Halloween in North America, is devoted to *los angelitos* (little angels), for whom there is a night vigil and a blessing the following morning. After this ceremony, All Saints' Day is dedicated to the deceased adults. Their *ofrendas* are more elaborate, with spicier foods, the personal clothes, and favorite cigarettes of the deceased, and even alcoholic beverages. On 2 November, All Souls' Day, there is often a mass to honor all the dead and a household trek to the cemetery to pray for the dead. That afternoon and evening, households often hold their most ceremonial meal, at which presents are exchanged and family solidarities are renewed. At the end of the dinner, at least in more traditional households, there is a farewell ritual (La Despedida) of prayers and rosaries for the departing souls.

These are the most formal, intimate, and respectful aspects of Dias de Muertos. But the more public manifestations of the fiesta are more raucous, light-hearted, and humorous. As Rosalind Beimler explains, "The Days of the Dead are celebrated with a mixture of reverence for the departed, revelry to make them happy upon their return, and mockery to defy the fear of death itself."[23] Mexicans "obstinately refuse to take death seriously," remarks Gonzalez-Crussi. On the Day of the Dead, the European *danse macabre* becomes literally and metaphorically a "frenzied *zapateado*, with all in attendance clapping, hooting, and joining the dance." The "skeleton leads the way and nobody seems to be surprised," for the Mexican way of death is characterized by "merry-making and fatalistic impassiveness."[24]

This exuberance for life in the face of death was remarked upon by Eisenstein in the 1930s:

> Food and drink are consumed, fireworks are lit (in broad daylight!) alternating with that traditional expression of joy—pistol shooting, carousels whirl around, stalls and puppet shows do a roaring trade, and on top of the gravestones in the cemetery, amid the burnt stubs of candles and crepe-festooned portraits of the deceased brought from home, men and women strive to ensure that the human race shall not die out.[25]

Pictorially, this zest for life is best captured in the woodcuts and engravings of José Luis Guadalupe Posada. Building on the comical epitaphs that sometimes characterized the European All Souls', and upon a spirited street culture that sometimes transformed the Day of the Dead into a "vulgar show" of "Gothic and Vandal theater,"[26] Posada created a buoyant urban vernacular art form that satirized Mexican society of the late nineteenth and early twentieth century. In his mock epitaphs, or *calaveras,* as they were called, with their grinning skulls and puppet-like skeletons, Posada spared neither rich nor poor, banker nor bandit with the "penetrating edge of his chisel."[27] On the Day of the Dead, Posada portrayed "vivid and lively skeletons and skulls with grinning teeth, dancing, cycling, playing the guitar, plying their trades, drinking, masquerading," or, like the rakish *vaquero* (cowboy) in his broad-rimmed hat and modish pants, picking up a young woman in the street.[28] Whereas the traditional *danse macabre* warned and instructed people that worldly distinctions were superficial and transitory because death was always round the corner, Posada's woodcuts portrayed the exuberance of life in the face of death. Whereas the medieval convention

Calaveras living it up, by José Luis Guadalupe Posada, early twentieth century.

tended to be pompously preachy, Posada's was defiant and parodic. As Diego Rivera put it, death in Posada's work was "personified as a skeleton that gets drunk, picks fights, sheds tears and dances for joy."[29] Death itself was mocked, not simply the pretensions of the living.

Whether Posada's vision of *El Dia de los Muertos* has promoted an existential attitude toward death that displaced older Christian and pre-Christian notions of mortality is an issue on which commentators cannot agree. The issue was dramatically posed by Octavio Paz in his well-known book *The Labyrinth of Solitude*. He argued that the popular Day of the Dead images affirmed "the nothingness and insignificance of human existence." In his view, the modern Mexican joked about death, "caresses it, sleeps with it, celebrates it" and "looks at it, face to face, with impatience, disdain or irony."[30] In the light of these observations, anthropologists have reexamined the religious meanings of the Day of the Dead with a new curiosity. Following Paz, Stanley Brandes has recently argued that "the iconography of death holds virtually no sacred meaning either for its producers or its consumers."[31] By contrast, Juanita Garciagodoy believes that behind the mocking tone of the *calaveras* there is a fatalism about death that rests on a bedrock of Christian and Mesoamerican belief about the afterlife. She observes that contemporary Mexicans continue to believe that the spirits can effectively intercede with the saints on behalf of living friends and relatives.[32]

Perhaps both notions coexist in a country of "multiple historical levels," to quote the novelist and critic Carlos Fuentes, where secular linear time and the dream of modernity itself has been only partially achieved—historically, at the expense of the communitarian culture of peasant and indigenous peoples.[33] Whether this observation is pertinent or not to the seeming plurality of attitudes toward death that prevail in contemporary Mexico, it is clear that Posada's celebration of the fiesta has had a profound influence on its modern manifestations. In Mexican shops and stalls, sugar skulls beam at consumers, skeletons advertise *panes de muerto*, and skeletal marionettes and papier mâché *calaveras* confront death by parodying life. In the spirit of Posada, *calaveras* or *calacas*, small figurines sold in markets as gifts or decorations, mock the pretensions of modern, especially bourgeois life, the fragility of modern technology, and the ups-and-downs of marriage. In newspapers, mock-epitaphs depict the heads of politicians in skull and crossbones, with verses satirizing their activities and false promises.[34]

The Day of the Dead, then, is not simply a reverential holiday. It is a holiday that retains reverential moments or ritual spaces for families who can connect with past memories and reaffirm and reconfigure their own personal histories. But, like many festivals, it is also a site of social and political commentary, with an irreverent side. As historian William Beezley has noted, the Day of the Dead has conventionally offered ordinary people the opportunity to express their dissatisfactions with political leaders and to voice their grievances.[35]

In this respect it is not unlike Halloween, although there are some obvious differences. The Day of the Dead is definitely a more family-centered holiday, embracing all ages and generations. It is a festival devoted to preserving familial oral memories. In North America, this is more likely to happen, if it happens at all, at Christmas, Passover, Easter, or Thanksgiving than at Halloween. In its modern version, Halloween is only family-centered at one particular moment in the family life-cycle: when small children are costumed and accompanied on their trick-or-treating rituals by family members. Even this familial ritual, I have suggested, is on the decline in the wake of Halloween sadist scares.

Yet modern-day Halloween does bear some concordance with the more public side of the Day of the Dead. Halloween allows festive space for social criticism and parody, as does the Day of the Dead, although it lacks the institutional form of the mock epitaphs, which provide the Mexican holiday with a more permanent forum of dissent. Children "beg" on Halloween in much the same way as do urban Mexican children on the Day of the Dead. Whereas North American children trick-or-treat, Mexican children, following older All Souls' rituals, parade the streets with candles in cardboard boxes, asking passers-by for money for their *calaveras*. Halloween is arguably more of a street masquerade than the Day of the Dead, with an abundance of costumes depicting a wide variety of themes. And yet on the Day of the Dead, masked revelers congregate at bars and discos in Mexican City and other large urban centers. In some rural villages such as Zapotitla in Hidalgo, men even dress as women in a masked dance of death that moves from house to house in a manner analogous to earlier forms of Halloween mummery.[36]

Not surprisingly in this era of NAFTA, there has been some crossover between the two festivals. Witches and pumpkins adorn Mexican window displays, and orange balloons and jack-o'-lanterns decorate urban gravestones and *ofrendas*. Children in Mexico City demand their *"jaloguin"* (Halloween treats) from door to door, perhaps scrawling *"codos"* ("skinflints") on the walls of those who refuse to shell out. The

Death visits the
Halloween Masquer
Aid, Toronto, 1998.
Photo by Nick Rogers.

wealthy urbanites of Mexico even take their children to Halloween
costume parties, symbolically identifying, no doubt, with ambitious,
successful Americans. Across the border, Day of the Dead motifs saturate
the Celebration of Life festival at the Heard Museum in Phoenix; *panes
de muertos* become the rage in San Antonio; and street processions in
towns like San Juan Bautista, California, draw vim from the skeletal
performers of the Teatro Campesino (Rural Theatre Group).[37] Taking
their cue from Latino communities, other religious congregations have
also adopted the practice of cleaning up and adorning their gravesites

on All Saints' or All Souls' Day. In Texas and South Carolina, even some mainstream Protestant denominations have adopted this liturgical calendar to commemorate and pray for the dead.[38] In a North American culture that all too often tries to hide and sanitize death, the conventions of the Day of the Dead seem a healthy antidote. One correspondent writing in the *New York Times* in the immediate aftermath of the terrorist attack upon the World Trade Center urged readers to transform the upcoming Halloween into a day of remembrance similar to that of the Day of the Dead. Halloween "need not be a day of satire and horror," she observed, "but can instead be a chance to linger with those we miss while the veil between the worlds is so thin." She said she would put out flowers and candles at a small altar in memory of her father and sister who died years ago, as well as photographs of the twin towers.[39]

In the American Southwest, this exchange has been heralded as cultural tolerance or as a virtuous expression of multiculturalism. In Mexico, it is more often seen as a disturbing capitulation to American culture, sometimes insidiously sponsored by the Mexican elite. "It's interesting that the *clases populares* are not borrowing directly from the U.S. but from the wealthier, urban classes," remarked George Rabasa. "So in a sense it's a case of imitating the customs of their 'betters,' adding a level of worldliness and stylishness to the altars and *panteon* decorations."[40] Whether this is the case or not, it is clear that the incorporation of Halloween motifs into Day of the Dead celebrations is part of a larger debate about the benefits of NAFTA for Mexicans, and the complicity of the country's dominant classes in the modernizing project. In this respect, the significance of mock epitaphs that conventionally satirize the pretensions of the rich takes on new political overtones. Since Dias de Muertos is commonly regarded as integral to Mexico's national and cultural identity, its bourgeoisie can be seen as sell-outs.[41]

What also brings an urgency to the debate over the corrosive influence of Halloween on Todos Santos is the fact that the Mexican fiesta has become increasingly commercialized. Mexican celebrations of the

"Thinking of You." A contemporary Day of the Dead greeting card, New Mexico.

Day of the Dead are now tourist attractions, particularly on the island of Janitzio on Lake Patzcuaro and in the nearby town of Tzintzuntuan. This is also the case in the valley of Oaxaca; tour companies offer four-night packages to Monte Alban and Mitla.[42] Since the 1980s, states such as Tlaxcala have also sponsored competitions for the most artistic *ofrendas*, again to attract visitors to the event. These promotional efforts have gone hand in hand with an abridgement and decline of the traditional rituals of the Day of the Dead. In rural Tlaxcala, for example, only 35 percent of all households observe all the traditional rituals surrounding the holiday. Most spend less time decorating their *ofrendas* and observing their vigils than did their ancestors a generation before. Clearly, Mexican anxieties about Halloween are in part a reflection of the commercial and secularizing forces influencing Mexico's own holiday.

In the current political context, these anxieties are understandable, although they ignore the extent to which the Day of the Dead is itself an "invented tradition," one that has been modified over the centuries, not least at the hands of Jose Luis Guadalupe Posada. There is room, one might argue, for the accommodation of Halloween into this rich, syncretic festival, as there has been for other symbols of American popular culture such as Superman, the latter giving rise to a real-life character called Superbarrio.[43] One recent Mexico City window display by Carlos Oznaya, entitled "Merienda exquisita" (Delicious Supper), portayed a male and female *calavera* salivating at the huge *pan de muerto* on the table. Amid the salacious talk of licking this "deliciousness" and "getting it up," the scantily clad, well-endowed female sits on two jack-o'-lanterns, both of whom want a piece of the bread (or the action).[44] The larger pumpkin squeals to the couple: "Stop being self-important . . . and give me my part." The positioning of the pumpkins is significant. They are voyeurs to the feast, not part of it. Like the marzipan pumpkins upon which smiling skeletons sit in the window of Mexico City's leading candy store, Halloween plays a subordinate role in the Day of the Dead's reconfiguration; how harmonious a role remains to be seen.

๏ 8 ๏

Halloween
at the Millennium

Halloween at the millennium is a contested and in many respects a controversial holiday. There is little consensus as to what it means or to how it should be observed. To be sure, Halloween still retains some vestigial links to the harvest. Its pumpkins and apples are part of the festive fare of harvest suppers and thanksgiving dinners. Newspapers and magazines routinely provide tips around Halloween as to how these seasonal fruits and vegetables might be enjoyed. *Martha Stewart Living* magazine produced a Halloween edition in 2000 in which the festive fare was scary yet upscale, with garlic soup, devil's salsa, and pretzels in the shape of severed fingers with ladylike red almond "nails." But it also featured mulled apple cider and reminded readers of the close association of Halloween with the end of the harvest in nineteenth-century America.[1] In some places, of course, this seasonal association is still critical. In the rural areas of the American Northeast, for example, Halloween continues to be a marker of the hunting season, a time when farmers open their land to hunters, hikers, and snowmobilers.[2]

Yet beyond this, there is not much agreement. Despite the razor-in-the-apple scares and the rumors of contaminated candies, many people cling to a vision of Halloween as a preeminently children's festival. They

Halloween and the
harvest: the scarecrow
and pumpkin on the
porch. *Photo by Nick
Rogers.*

would no doubt be relieved to hear that in 1996, fourteen years after
the Tylenol scare, the proportion of U.S. households distributing treats
had risen to a respectable 78 percent.[3] Whether this will revitalize trick-
or-treating or whether it will continue to falter in the light of the current
anthrax scares remains to be seen. The ritual is still seen in some quarters
as an important expression of neighborhood solidarity, even as inner-
city neighborhoods gentrify or crumble and upscale residential districts
are walled off from intruders. Many people continue to believe that
Halloween costuming allows children the opportunity to be fanciful,
to indulge their imaginations in a familiar setting, and perhaps to come
to terms with the sinister in warm and secure surroundings. As Michele
Slung and Roland Hartman have suggested, Halloween can be viewed
as a "chance to put just a touch of mystery, a little 'safe' danger, into the
humdrum fabric of our lives." In their view, Halloween has become a
"national moment dedicated to the weird."[4]

In some households, Halloween has been integrated into an annual ritual of familial gatherings, whether they be midnight hayrides, pumpkin-carving parties, Halloween breakfasts before dawn, or decorating the house for haunted nights.[5] Even so, one of the main forces promoting Halloween as a children's festival is inevitably the school. Halloween parties and parades at school are an important fixture of the fall term, one of the first large festivals that children might experience outside their home environment. It is no accident that candy manufacturers begin to publicize their wares alongside "back-to-school" promotions. It is a seasonal opportunity too good to be missed: Halloween-related products generated sales of $950 million in 1998 and $2 billion by 2000. "Every year," remarked a spokesman for the U.S. National Retail Federation, "there are more market tie-ins from cookies to breakfast cereals to Taco Bell."[6] Whether it is Nabisco's Ghastly Gummies, black and orange Jell-O, or boxes of chocolate cookies embossed with pictures of Frankenstein, Dracula, and the Wolfman, Halloween is big business in the snack and candy industry. Candies not only help consolidate Halloween's current status as a children's festival, but they also prepare children for festive consumption from an early age. As Leigh Schmidt, a professor of religion at Princeton has recently emphasized, the shopping bag has become the archetypal trick-or-treat symbol, signifying "little shoppers in the making."[7]

Food manufacturers may savor the monster marketing opportunities opened by Halloween, but celebrating the holiday at school has become a controversial business. In recent years, Right-to-Lifers have objected to UNICEF collections in schools on the grounds that it supports groups that advocate abortion. Christian fundamentalists have also taken exception to Halloween school parties on the grounds that they insidiously promote pagan, if not satanic, beliefs. There have been attempts to ban the annual party outright, or at the very least to prevent masquerading as devils and witches. In Peachtree City, Georgia, children are not allowed to dress up in any costume that might evoke satanic imagery; rather, they are urged to celebrate "Book-Character

Dress-Up Day."[8] Mickey Mouse might be okay, but sympathy with the devil is not.

The religious Right has generally not made much headway on this score, largely because, in the United States especially, censorship of this kind flouts cherished freedoms of expression. As a correspondent to the *Atlanta Constitution* admitted, Halloween may have begun as a pagan festival, but in the United States it was now a "festival of fun, feasts, fancy frocks, and frivolous fright. Ours is not just a Christian nation," the writer explained, "but a nation born from the search for religious freedom. Let the kids have some fun."[9] In the light of this attitude, which commands widespread support, efforts to ban Halloween in schools have failed in the face of community protests.[10]

As a result, religious sects have thought of ways of appropriating the holiday in their own idioms. Some churchgoers dress their children in "happy" attire for the annual trick-or-treat, rather than in the ghoulish garb that conventionally marks the ritual. One mother from Colesville Baptist Church in the Washington area had her six children pass out religious tracts as they received candies. "Halloween has its dark side," she remarked, "but we turn it around to beat the Devil."[11] Other evangelicals have sponsored Hallelujah Nights or Harvest Festivals as a counterpoint to Halloween. The Southpointe Baptist Fellowship in Leesburg, Florida, staged a Christian alternative to Halloween in 2001 that featured Bible-based games, a cookout, a cake walk, and face painting.[12] A few years ago, the Ebenezer AME Church in Fort Washington organized a "Holyween," in which revelers were asked to dress as characters from the Bible or the civil rights movement and to explain their character's contribution to history. As the senior pastor of the church explained: "We really wanted to change the focus of Halloween from ghosts and goblins and things that are evil to a spiritual focus."[13]

If Biblical narratives and characters have sometimes been substituted for the traditional Halloween motifs, haunted houses have been renovated to highlight the dangers of a permissive society. Since 1990, the Trinity Christian School in Cedar Hill, Texas, has organized a Hell House to give local teenagers a "reality check" to the dangers of today's mainstream culture. These dangers are defined as drug-ridden raves, sex before marriage, homosexuality, family violence, and school shootings such as the one at Columbine. In the hyperbolic dramas that Trinity members enact for their largely petrified or bewildered audiences, to judge from the recent documentary film on the Hell House, these Pentecostal Christians mobilize fear of damnation to scare teenagers into the paths of righteousness. According to the film, of the 75,000 who have visited the Hell House since it opened, 15,000 have joined the church.[14]

In the wake of this success, other evangelical churches have promoted similar scare-fare enterprises on Halloween as a counterpoint to society's permissiveness. In 1996, a church in Arvada, Colorado, sponsored a Hell House to drive home to its visitors the evils of alternative life-styles and drink, much in the style of the Cedar Hill enterprise. In the first room, a man dies of AIDS; in the second, a woman writhes from an abortion; in the third, a young woman dies from a toxic cocktail of drugs and alcohol; in the fourth, a drunk driver has killed his family. Finally, having passed through a hell reeking of Limburger cheese, visitors are blessed by Jesus and saved. Such exhibitions are strenuously defended as a "death-defyin', Satan-be-cryin' . . . cutting-edge evangelism tool of the 90s."[15]

The evangelical denunciation of Halloween as a conduit of permissive values has inevitably brought it into conflict with other groups. While Wiccans have protested that Halloween can be a spiritual day of renewal and remembrance, gay activists have resented the attempt to restrict their exhibitionism on the holiday. In San Francisco, in particular, there have been angry confrontations with the Christian Right over the drag promenades on Castro and Polk Streets. Thus far, the champions of alternative sexualities have won the day. Not only are gay organizations politically powerful in many metropolitan cities; the street parades in which they participate have become tourist fixtures. The Greenwich

Village Halloween parade now attracts over a million spectators every year, many of them visitors, and infuses an estimated $60 million into the local economy.[16] Confronted with this sort of commercial bonanza, many civic leaders are prepared to wink at the carnivalesque excesses of Halloween night, even if they are troubled by its significations. Halloween is a $700 million enterprise in Canada, and in the United States, where an average family spends $45 on Halloween and twenty-year-olds a good deal more, it now grosses $6.8 billion, having more than doubled its revenue from candy, costumes, cards, and party supplies in the last five years. This figure does not include commercial tie-ins offered by fast-food chains or automobile salesmen.[17]

Halloween is currently the second most important party night in North America. In terms of its retail potential, it is second only to Christmas. This commercialism fortifies its significance as a time of public license, a custom-designated opportunity to have a blast. As one Washington journalist has remarked, it is "a conduit for all of us to let off a little steam."[18] Clearly, some people are unhappy about this, especially the temperance and religious groups who decry the heavy advertising of the beer companies on Halloween and the celebration of same-sex coupling that accompanies many of the large urban parades and celebrations.[19] In the voracious appropriation of space that this festival encourages, there is plenty of room for the play of difference and the parody of the orthodox, practices that are deeply troubling to more traditional folk.

Yet Halloween can also be seen as a homogenizing force, as the epitome of North American mass culture. It is now over a hundred years since Halloween could be described as an ethnic festival, and while it never became part of the fabric of state-sponsored holidays, it is sufficiently part of the mainstream to represent American-ness. Since the second decade of the twentieth century, Halloween was among the commercial red-letter days of the American calendar, with advertisements publicizing its cards and accessories. It is not surprising that in today's global economy, Halloween should be exported abroad, to South

America, Europe, and even the Far East. Halloween has made a very visible comeback in Britain, even in places where it is no longer part of popular memory. In corner shops across this country, Halloween masks and candies are now for sale in late October, alongside the fireworks for Bonfire Night. In many parts of England, trick-or-treating has taken hold, and Halloween pranks are becoming commonplace. In 2001, there were press reports of teenagers throwing eggs and flour at passing automobiles and obstructing roads with fallen trees.[20] The pranks might be regarded in England as part of an indigenous tradition of youthful reveling, now no longer confined to Bonfire Night, but the trick-or-treating, candies, and costumes are more obviously American imports. The same is true of the attempt to introduce Halloween to Japan under the auspices of the Japanese Biscuit Association.[21] In this respect, Halloween International is not unlike McDonald's and Coca-Cola.

Halloween is not a particularly contentious holiday among immigrants in North America, although its flagrant commercialism and exhibitionism might offend some on religious or cultural grounds. It is only in the Southwest and Mexico that Halloween poses a major problem of national and ethnic identity, in the border zone where the two different festivals meet. In this zone, Halloween is regarded as a marker of Anglo identity. In Mexico, especially, it is seen as one manifestation of an American capitalism that is corroding indigenous Mexican traditions. As I have argued, this view overlooks both the commercial promotion of the Day of the Dead and the fiesta's capacity to absorb new elements within it. Even so, it is clear that Halloween is quite distinct from the Day of the Dead, in both its secularism and its symbolism. Halloween is quite shamelessly secular, without any explicit Christian referent to the souls in purgatory with which it was first associated. Jack-o'-lanterns may commemorate, at some vestigial level, the wandering souls of purgatory, but hardly anyone acknowledges or understands this historical referent. More often than not, carved pumpkins and Halloween masks celebrate the grotesque and macabre, the weird and the scary. Halloween is interested in the afterlife only as a mode of transgression or repression, as a means of probing and coming to terms with modern-day fears and anxieties. Its modern or postmodern trajectory has been toward the Gothic rather than the Christian notion of death.

How one celebrates Halloween, then, is very much an individual choice, and one that has given rise to considerable controversy about the limits of permissiveness, the boundaries of transgression, the propagation of sexual difference, the role Halloween plays in propagating the "American way of life," and the adult appropriation of what many still conceive as a children's festival of fantasy. Normally, the battle over what Halloween should be has taken place in local contexts, at least within North America. But in 2001, in the wake of the terrorist attacks on the World Trade Center and the Pentagon, the discussion became more self-consciously national in scope (at least in the United States). Just how gory and frivolously unwholesome should Halloween be in the face of Ground Zero? Should children be allowed to trick-or-treat amid anthrax scares and fears of further terrorist attacks? Or should Halloween's history be reappropriated as a festival of mourning and

Jack-o'-lantern beaming in the night. *Photo by Nick Rogers.*

loss? Could North Americans learn something from the Dia de los Muertos south of the Rio Grande? These were some of the questions haunting Halloween in its first test of the millennium.

For a few commentators, the events of 11 September were an opportunity to change the character of Halloween, to recover its historic roots as a feast honoring the dead.[22] For others, it was an opportunity to blend the Anglo-American festival with the Mexican. Louisa Rocha-McCarthy, a translator from Portland, Maine, who had experienced both holidays since her youth, believed that the Mexican holiday had much to offer as a way of coping with loss and urged readers to consider its relevance in the current conjuncture. Martha Klein agreed. In a letter to the *New York Times*, written one month after the World Trade Center disaster, she reported that she had

> experienced the Day of the Dead in Mexico several times, and was deeply moved at the heartfelt and, yes, sometimes joyous altars and ceremonies there. Halloween and All Souls' Day are experienced there as an opportunity to spend time with those who are gone. My altar in my home this year will again include pictures of my father and sister, whom I lost years ago, as well as images of the twin towers and whatever other pictures, flowers and candles I need to honor those who died in our tragedy. We have been horrified and terrified enough, and perhaps can use this holiday as a chance to continue our individual and collective healing.[23]

This multicultural perspective was echoed in parts of the Southwest. In Laredo, Texas, where the Mexican Day of the Dead is robustly celebrated alongside Halloween, a memorial to the victims of the terrorist attack was erected at the local Center for the Arts. In San Antonio, too, artists honored the victims at a public *ofrenda*.[24] Yet elsewhere in the United States, Halloween was distanced from the Day of the Dead in what at best could be a recognition of cultural diversity.

For the majority, the real issue was whether Halloween should be celebrated in conventional ways, or how it might be accented in the aftermath of 11 September, when panic and despondency were rife.

The mood of the country was affected by premonitions of further terrorist attacks. One of the rumors that surfaced on the Internet concerned an Afghani or Arab who disappeared before 11 September but warned his girlfriend not to fly on that fated day or to frequent a mall on Halloween. The FBI investigated and publicly discounted the story, but the purported communicator of it, one Laura Katsis of Volt Information Services in California, was bombarded with calls and e-mail queries. In fact, the tale quickly assumed the status of an urban legend in cyberspace and prompted mall operators as far afield as Maine to abandon their traditional Halloween activities or at the very least to step up local security.[25] What heightened the anxiety were the reports of anthrax contamination, a matter that inevitably raised the specter of another crazed Halloween similar to those of the early 1980s, when cyanide-tainted candies loomed large in the public imagination. Some areas of the United States became so jumpy that even straightforward pro-motional activities were misinterpreted. When the Littleton-based Village Homes mailed pumpkin seeds to over 11,000 Arvada, Colorado, residents for a pumpkin-patch event in aid of the New York firefighters, a number of recipients contacted the police, worried that the lump in their orange-colored envelopes might be a biohazard. As the marketing director of Village Homes admitted, "the timing couldn't have been worse."[26]

Predictably, these tales brought out Halloween's detractors. The holiday should have been banned. It promoted phoney scares that encouraged national paranoia, if not paralysis—exactly what terrorists wanted. It was a ghoulish extravagance that was totally inappropriate to the current circumstances, when Americans needed to come to terms with the real horrors of terrorism, not with fake body parts and gore. In the call for a revivified nation in the wake of the attacks, Halloween seemed to some to be little more than a baby-boomer bonanza, at once insular, self-indulgent, and decadent. It was time that children, the purported beneficiaries of Halloween, learned the virtues of sacrifice, not the conventions of mindless consumerism. "Take the dough you'd spend on Halloween candy," remarked Kevin Horrigan in the *St. Louis Post-Dispatch*, "and send it to the Red Cross. The president wants kids to each send $1 to the Red Cross. How 'bout $1.9 billion instead?"[27]

The response to these objections ran as follows. In the current economic context in which terrorism has harmed the economy, consumerism is patriotism. The show must go on, not only because Halloween is a $6 billion retail extravaganza that could boost economic confidence, but because "business as usual" is the real psychological antidote to terrorism. Halloween is an American tradition that should be honored. Banning or severely restricting Halloween was wimpy, unpatriotic, and ideologically un-American.[28] It would "cheapen" the deaths of the World Trade Center victims, claimed one correspondent in the *St. Louis Post*.[29] Although at least one state governor advised citizens to tone down their celebrations in the interests of national safety and the capabilities of the security services, others were more defiant. Angus King, the governor of Maine, remarked that bioterrorists could "mess up the postal service, but they had better stay away from trick-or-treating."[30] Celebrating Halloween in the "traditional way" could be a confidence booster, it was argued, a significant scenario in a return to normalcy. "Halloween is an important holiday in our country," remarked Timothy Chanaud of Paramount's Scream Factory, "and enjoying Halloween is part of the return to normal life. Halloween is supposed to be scary. It's about fantasy. People look for that kind of escape from the real world."[31] Whether one bought this line or not, many parents certainly felt that Halloween would provide their children with a wholesome continuity in troubled times. "Rituals for kids shouldn't change," remarked one Californian; "Halloween is part of our culture." Or as one mother of seven from Utah put it, whose own mother was killed in the World Trade Center attack: "The kids need something to be afraid of that they can control. The kids can control Halloween-scary; it's not real, like the other."[32]

If the dominant mood in the United States was to stand firm for the familiar, some things did change in the celebration of Halloween in 2001. Trick-or-treating declined amid anthrax scares, by as much as 30 percent in some areas. Shopping malls did close. In the Chicago area, General Growth Properties banned trick-or-treating and other Halloween events in its 145 shopping centers.[33] Where such centers remained open, security was increased and toy guns and masks were prohibited.[34]

According to the National Retail Federation, total expenditures on Halloween in 2001 declined by 17 percent. They were noticeably higher only among some costume shops and distributors and among some craft suppliers, a fact that suggests that some Americans decided to celebrate Halloween this year in a more domestic setting and avoid the potential hazards of mall crawls or trick-or-treating.

In keeping with this spirit, what was worn or exhibited also changed. Alice Cooper may have toted the mock severed head of Britney Spears after her brief appearance on his Halloween tour,[35] but the old '70s rocker was bucking the trend. Generally speaking, gore was out in 2001. There were fewer dismembered body parts on display, fewer fountains of blood. And off-color jokes about being "gored" or "bushwhacked" were discouraged.[36] "A nation that recently suffered the worst terrorist attack in history and is now scared by the sight of sherbet powder," remarked one newspaper, "has little appetite for imitation horror."[37] Bloodbath Underground at Universal Studios, Florida, was renamed the Ooze Zone Fright Club. Paramount's Scream Factory toned down its blood and guts. Schools asked parents to refrain from providing their children with masks that were excessively gory or with costumes that featured dismembered bodies. They were particularly anxious to ban the push-button rubber masks that spurted blood.[38] Lest the "reality effects" be too easily associated with the tragedy at Ground Zero, Six Flags Marine World in Sacramento changed the name of its Terror Train to Ghost Train, "terror" having become an overly emotive signifier. Similarly, the owner of a Fright

House in Washington canceled the "Escape from the Pentagon" section for "ethical and moral reasons."[39]

U.S. citizens abandoned gore for more patriotic motifs in 2001. The best-selling costumes for adults were Uncle Sam and the Statue of Liberty, sometimes fashionably cut to expose the midriff. George Washington, Abe Lincoln, and Civil War soldiers were also popular. Among children, firefighter, pilot, police, and soldier costumes sold well, as did Superman, Batman, the conventional Disney characters, and the topical Harry Potter. Overall, people were looking for a "kinder and gentler Halloween"[40] and were quite prepared to mix the seasonal black and orange with the national red, white, and blue. Some places went out of their way to exploit Halloween as a promoter of patriotism. In Richmond, Virginia, a "Show Your Spirit" fancy-dress contest was organized with a top prize of $1000.[41] Red, white, and blue was de rigueur. A similar spirit swept through the schools. At Allenwood Elementary School in Temple Hills, Maryland, for example, children were encouraged to wear red, white, and blue outfits and to wrap flags around their heads. In the actual festivities, they recited the pledge of allegiance and sang "God Bless America" before releasing red, white, and blue balloons into the sky.[42] Similarly, the thirty-third annual children's Halloween parade of the Venice Lions Club featured youngsters waving the Stars and Stripes. In Wyoming, one school organized a "Hero-ween" celebration to honor the New York police and fire departments, believing that kids wanted to "be part of the healing process as well."[43] For those with a more international perspective, "God bless America" celebrations were sometimes accompanied by contributions to Afghani children.[44]

Even adult parades contained their fair share of patriotic boosterism. Although a few outrageous costumes were noted in Hollywood, where one reveler offered a parody of "Miss Afghanistan" in a skimpy two-piece camouflage outfit that exposed the midriff, the fancy-dress promenades were generally less gory, less provocative, and more patriotic.[45] In New York, the Greenwich Village Parade, hitherto known for its radical nonconformity, centered on the theme of rebirth, the Phoenix rising from the ashes. In Austin, Texas, angels with red, white, and blue wings mingled with firefighters, Marines, and Uncle Sam on stilts. Although a few people in Arabian garb were reported, Middle Eastern costumes were in short supply. Some retailers refused to sell them, fearing they would incite violence. Osama bin Laden masks, popular in Mexico City and Rio de Janeiro, were virtually impossible to buy in the United States.[46] Many distributors refused to stock them. Even so, Lady Liberty could be found parading bin Laden's head in Pittsburgh, and at the Haunted Railway in Salt Lake City, it was possible to fling coins at his dummy.[47] In Cuyahoga Falls, Ohio, bin Laden was found in a coffin, displacing Dracula as the monster of the season.[48] In contrast, the most popular masks in the United States were those of George Bush, the President who demanded bin Laden "dead or alive" and urged citizens to continue "business as usual," and Rudy Giuliani, the mayor who soothed nerves, handled disaster with dignity, and pledged the reconstruction of America's most devastated city.

The year 2001 was arguably the first time that Halloween was self-consciously appropriated for patriotic purposes in America. This is of some significance, since Halloween has conventionally been seen as a populist counterfestival, a holiday that conventionally presumed no abiding pledges of solidarity nor reverential lineages. This legacy explained its popularity in the nineteenth and twentieth century. Halloween grew outside the canon of state-sanctioned commemorative holidays. It was a rite without a patron, eluding institutional or corporate appropriation, a holiday of transgression whose subversive laughter struck against the orthodoxies of the day and potentially, at least, challenged its social hierarchies, if only in a youthful, anarchic way.

Did 2001 mark the development of a different Halloween, one that might take its place alongside the Fourth of July as a preeminently patriotic festival? It is clearly too early to say, but I would suggest that it is highly unlikely. Over time, Halloween has been a fixed festival that can be accented in different ways, and following the tragedy of 2001, it was given a definite patriotic twist in the United States, although not in Canada. But it does not follow that this signals a new departure in the character of the holiday. Halloween belongs to an age in which festivals devoted to the nation-state have increasingly given way to a proliferation of commemorative practices devoted to all manner of causes.[49] As a rite without a patron, a festival without definitive referents, Halloween is well placed to survive in this postmodern context. But if the year 2001 tells us anything, it is that Halloween is now fundamentally part of the leisure industry. In the end, what mattered most about Halloween was whether it would fulfill its commercial potential in the threat of an economic recession, not whether Halloween would boost national morale or fund destitute Afghani children.

Ultimately, then, Halloween's significance in mainstream debate in 2001 resided in its retail potential, not in its potential for social transgression. This was hardly surprising, given the extraordinary circumstances in which it was celebrated. But it might be reasonable to ask whether this will be a portent of the future. The question is worth pondering, because in the past Halloween has sometimes proved to be a useful site for promoting different ways of seeing the world. As a borderline, liminal festival, Halloween has sponsored social inversion and subversive laughter. At its most critical it has approximated what the French philosopher Michel Foucault would call a heterotopia, a countersite from which the extravagancies and pretensions of modern-day life, the rules regulating sexuality, could be parodied and openly questioned.[50] Admittedly, Halloween time, like festive time in general, is fleeting, transitory, and precarious, generating spaces that are themselves decentered and highly individualized. And admittedly, the dominant tropes of Halloween, humor and play, tend to parody power and mock its pretensions rather than subvert it in any fundamental way. But will Halloween lose even this social edge as it increasingly becomes big business? Will it be so deeply enmeshed in consumer culture that its counterhegemonic energies will be easily accommodated, appropri-ated, or dissipated? Perhaps it is too early to tell. It will depend on how inventive people can be in bending this carnivalesque consumer rite to express their own desires, dissatisfactions, and fantasies.

ᴨ⊙TES

Introduction

1. On this episode, see Gary Kates, *Monsieur d'Eon Is a Woman* (New York: Basic Books, 1995); Anna Clark, "The Chevalier D'Eon and Wilkes: Masculinity and Politics in the Eighteenth Century," *Eighteenth-Century Studies* 32 (1998): 19–48.

2. *U.S. News and World Report* 123/17 (3 Nov. 1997): 14; *Florida Times*, 15 Oct. 2001, p. B1, citing figures from the National Retail Federation.

3. Ronald Hutton, *The Stations of the Sun* (Oxford: Oxford University Press, 1996), 382–83; Charles Kightly, *The Customs and Ceremonies of Britain* (New York: Thames and Hudson, 1986), 191.

4. Cf. Jack Kugelmass, *Masked Culture: The Greenwich Village Halloween Parade* (New York: Columbia University Press, 1994), 165.

Chapter 1: Samhain and the Celtic Origins of Halloween

1. Cited in Hutton, *Stations of the Sun*, 361.

2. J. A. MacCulloch, *The Religion of the Ancient Celts* (Edinburgh: T. and T. Clark, 1911), 263.

3. Hutton, *Stations of the Sun*, 361.

4. *Maclean's Magazine* 109/44 (28 Oct. 1996): 14.

5. *New York Times*, 27 Oct. 1996, p. E1.

6. See Jeffrey Burton Russell, "The Historical Satan," in James T. Richardson, Joel Best, and David G. Bromley, eds., *The Satanism Scare* (New York: A. de Gruyter, 1991), 41–48; Peter Stanford, *The Devil: A Biography* (New York: Heinemann, 1996); Carlo Ginzburg, *Ecstacies: Deciphering the Witches' Sabbath* (London: Hutchinson Radius, 1990).

7. Malcolm Chapman, *The Celts* (New York: St. Martin's Press, 1992), ch. 11.

8. Stuart Piggot, *The Druids* (London: Thames and Hudson, 1968), 110. For a full description, see T. D. Kendrick, *The Druids: A Study in Keltic Prehistory* (London: F. Cass, 1927), 89.

9. H. L. Jones, ed., *The Geography of Strabo*, 8 vols. (London: Loeb, 1979), 2: 247; C. H. Oldfather, ed., *Diodorus of Sicily*, 12 vols. (London: Loeb, 1970), 3: 179.

10. John Jackson, ed., *The Annals of Tacitus*, 3 vols. (London: Heinemann, 1981), 3: 157.

11. Julius Caesar, *The Gallic War*, ed. H. J. Edward (London: Loeb, 1986), 341. For Strabo's account, see *Geography*, 2: 249.

12. Piggot, *Druids*, 111; on the attribution of the sacrifice to Posidonius, see Ward Rutherford, *Celtic Lore* (London: HarperCollins, 1995), 84.

13. Strabo, *Geography*, 2: 245.

14. Geoffrey Keating, *A General History of Ireland*, 4 vols. (Dublin: Irish Texts Society, 1901), 4: 181. MacCulloch, *Ancient Celts*, 56–7, 80, implied that these tributes involved human sacrifice.

15. Rutherford, *Celtic Lore*, 97.

16. Peter Beresford Ellis, *The Druids* (London: Constable, 1994), 148–49.

17. For an account of the "Lindow Man," see Anne Ross and Don Robins, *The Life and Death of a Druid Prince* (New York: Summit Books, 1989). For skepticism about whether this was a ritual sacrifice, see Beresford Ellis, *Druids*, 152–53.

18. Piggott, *Druids*, 111–12.

19. Sir James Frazer, *The Golden Bough*, 13 vols. (London: Macmillan, 1911–36), 10: 225.

20. William Walsh, *Curiosities of Popular Customs* (Philadelphia: Lippincott, 1898), 501; see also the entry in the *New York Folklore Quarterly* 7/8 (1951–52): 321.

21. P. W. Joyce, *A Social History of Ancient Ireland*, 2 vols. (London: Longmans Green, 1903), 1: 251–52; MacCulloch, *Ancient Celts*, 51–52.

22. *Early Irish Myths and Sagas*, trans. Jeffrey Gantz (Harmondsworth, Middlesex: Penguin, 1981), 39.

23. Alwyn and Brinley Rees, *Celtic Heritage: Ancient Tradition in Ireland and Wales* (London: Thames and Hudson, 1961), 84.

24. Joyce, *Ancient Ireland*, 1: 265.

25. Caitlin Matthews and John Matthews, *The Encyclopaedia of Celtic Wisdom* (Shaftesbury, Dorset: Longmead, 1994), 118.

26. John King, *The Celtic Druids' Year* (London: Blandford, 1994).

27. On the concept of the liminal or liminality, see Victor Turner, *The Ritual Process* (London: Penguin, 1974), chs. 3–5, and *From Ritual to Theatre: The Human Seriousness of Play* (New York: Performing Arts Journal Publications, 1982), ch. 2.

28. Proinsias Mac Cana, *Celtic Mythology* (Feltham: Hamlyn, 1970), 127.

Chapter 2: Festive Rites

1. Edward Muir, *Ritual in Early Modern Europe* (Cambridge, Eng.: Cambridge University Press, 1997), 51.

2. William Carew Hazlitt, *Faiths and Folklore*, 2 vols. (London: Reeves and Turner, 1905), 1: 299; see also Ronald Hutton, *The Rise and Fall of Merrie England* (Oxford: Oxford University Press, 1994), 45.

3. R. Chambers, *The Book of Days: A Miscellany of Popular Antiquities*, 2 vols. (London: W. and R. Chambers, 1864), 2: 538; Georgina F. Jackson, *Shropshire Folk-Lore* (1883; rpt., Wakefield: EP Publishing, 1974), 379–80n. On the Mexican Day of the Dead, see Hugo Nutini, *Todos Santos in Rural Tlaxcala* (Princeton: Princeton University Press, 1988.)

4. Hutton, *Stations of the Sun*, 371.

5. William Shakespeare, *Two Gentlemen of Verona*, act II, scene 1.

6. Tusser, *Husbandry* (1878), 21: 55, noted in *OED*.

7. Nicholas Orme, "The Culture of Children in Medieval England," *Past and Present*, no. 148 (Aug. 1995): 96–97.

8. John Stow, *A Survay of London Written in the Year 1598*, ed. Henry Morley (London: Routledge, 1890), 123.

9. Philip Stubbs, *The Anatomy of Abuses in Ailgna* (London, 1583), 92–93. Also cited in Joseph Strutt, *A Complete View of the Dress and Habits of the People of England*, ed. J. R. Planche, 2 vols. (1842; rpt. London: Taband Press, 1970), 2: 200–201, with the addition of the shaming ritual, not mentioned in the original. See also Nicholas Rogers, "Halloween in Urban North America: Liminality and Hypperreality," *Histoire sociale/Social History*, 29 (1996): 464–65.

10. Natalie Zemon Davis, "The Reasons of Misrule," in *Society and Culture in Early Modern France* (Stanford: Stanford University Press, 1975), ch. 4; Jacques Le Goff and Jean-Claude Schmitt, eds., *Le Charivari* (New York: Mouton, 1981); Martin Ingram, "Ridings, Rough Music and the 'Reform of Popular Culture' in Early Modern England," *Past and Present*, no. 105 (Nov. 1984): 79–113; David Underdown, *Revel, Riot, and Rebellion* (Oxford: Clarendon Press, 1985), passim; E. P. Thompson, *Customs in Common* (London: Merlin Press, 1991), ch. 8.

11. Natalie Zemon Davis, "Charivari, Honor, and Community in Seventeenth-Century Lyon and Geneva," in Jack MacAloon, ed., *Rite, Drama, Festival, Spectacle* (Philadelphia: Institute for the Study of Human Issues, 1984), 42–57.

12. Davis, "Reasons of Misrule," 98, 105. For the reverential side of Hallowtide in France, see Maurice Vloberg, *Les fêtes de France: Coutumes religieuses et populaires* (Grenoble: B. Arthaud, 1936), 193–205.

13. Richard Crashaw, *The Poems*, ed. L. C. Martin (Oxford: Clarendon Press, 1957), 185.

14. Ms. 950: 170, Irish Folklore Collection, University College, Dublin (hereafter IFC Ms).

15. Christopher Haigh, "The Continuity of Catholicism in the English Reformation," in Haigh, ed., *The English Reformation Revisited* (Cambridge, Eng.: Cambridge University Press, 1987), 183; Hutton, *Merrie England*, 106–7.

16. Underdown, *Revel, Riot, and Rebellion*, 70.

17. *Gentleman's Magazine* 53 (1783): 578.

18. *Gentleman's Magazine* 54 (1784): 836.

19. David Cressy, *Birth, Marriage, and Death: Ritual, Religion, and the Life-Cycle in Tudor and Stuart England* (New York: Oxford University Press, 1997), 386.

20. Jackson, *Shropshire Folk-Lore*, 382.

21. Hutton, *Stations of the Sun*, 375; A. R. Wright, *British Calendar Customs: England*, ed. T. E. Jones, 3 vols. (London: Folklore Society, 1936–40), 2: 122.

22. On these doleing days, see Bob Bushaway, *By Rite: Custom, Ceremony and Community in England 1700–1880* (London: Junction Books, 1982), 167–90, 284.

23. T. F. Thiselton Dyer, *British Popular Customs, Past and Present* (London: G. Bell, 1876), 409, citing the *Journal of the Archaeological Association* 5 (1850): 253. See also Bushaway, *By Rite*, 183.

24. Charlotte S. Burne, "Souling, Clementing and Catterning: Three November Customs of the Western Midlands," *Folklore* 25 (1914): 285–99; Bushaway, *By Rite*, 183–86.

25. Samuel Bamford, *Autobiography*, ed. W. H. Chaloner, 2 vols. (London: Frank Cass, 1967), 2: 160–61. According to the Oxford English Dictionary, "Halloween" was first mentioned in print by the Scottish poet, Robert Ferguson, in 1773.

26. Thiselton Dyer, *British Popular Customs*, 395.

27. On the waning links between souling and All Souls' in nineteenth-century Yorkshire, see *Pub. Folklore Society* 45 (1899): 267.

28. Wright, *British Calendar Customs*, 3: 111, 117–19.

29. Ibid. 3: 112–13, 135.

30. Roy Palmer, *The Folklore of Leicestershire and Rutland* (Wymondham: Sycamore Press, 1985), 238; *British Press*, 14 Nov. 1820.

31. Wright, *British Calendar Customs*, 3: 155–56.

32. Thiselton Dyer, *British Popular Customs*, 414; *Pub. Folklore Society* 45 (1899): 268.

33. *Pub. Folklore Society* 63 (1908): 211.

34. Francis Place, *The Autobiography of Francis Place*, ed. Mary Thale (Cambridge, Eng.: Cambridge University Press, 1972), 65–66.

35. *Pub. Folklore Society* 64 (1911): 110–11.

36. Bushaway, *By Rite*, 64–76; Robert D. Storch, "'Please to Remember the Fifth of November': Conflict, Solidarity and Public Order in Southern England, 1815–1900," in Storch, ed., *Popular Culture and Custom in Nineteenth-Century England* (London and Canberra: Croom Helm, 1982), 71–99 (quote on p. 90); Wright, *British Calendar Customs*, 3: 155.

37. Palmer, *Folklore of Leicestershire*, 239.

38. Sue Ellen Thompson and Barbara W. Carlson, *Holidays, Festivals, and Celebrations of the World Dictionary* (Detroit: Omnigraphics, 1994), 208.

39. William Anderson, *No Ordinary Man: William Anderson's Edinburgh Journal* (Edinburgh: City of Edinburgh, 1986), 166.

40. Margo Todd, "Profane Pastimes and the Reformed Community: The Per-

sistence of Popular Festivities in Early Modern Scotland," *Journal of British Studies* 39 (April 2000): 123–56. See also Callum G. Brown, *Up-helly-aa: Custom, Culture and Community in Shetland* (Manchester: Mandolin Press, 1998), ch. 3.

41. *Scottish Voices 1745–1960*, eds., T. C. Smout and Sydney Wood (London: Collins, 1990), 170. Information on the 1940s and early 1950s provided by Professor Bill Dyck of the University of Toronto.

42. John Galt, *Ringan Gilhaize, or, the Covenanters*, ed. Patrick J. Wilson (1823; rpt., Edinburgh: Scottish Academic Press, 1984), 179.

43. Information from Drs. Roy Ritchie and John Short, both of whom celebrated Halloween in the Alloa, Dunfirmline, region in the 1950s.

44. Jacqueline R. Hill, "National Festivals, the State and 'Protestant Ascendancy' in Ireland, 1790–1829," *Irish Historical Studies* 24 (May 1984): 30–51; Niall O' Ciosáin, *Print and Popular Culture in Ireland 1750–1850* (London: Macmillan, 1997), 101; *Daily Gazetteer*, 20 Nov. 1735, where it is reported that the Boyne and Hanover clubs of Dublin celebrated the 1688 landing on 4 November.

45. Jack Santino, "Light Up the Sky: Halloween Bonfires and Cultural Hegemony in Northern Ireland," *Western Folklore* 55 (Spring 1996): 213–32.

46. Ibid.

47. IFC Ms. 950: 163.

48. IFC Ms. 949: 143–44.

49. IFC Ms. 949: 75

50. IFC Ms. 950: 225.

51. Mary Macleod Banks, *British Calendar Customs: Scotland*, 3 vols. (London: Folklore Society, 1937–41), 3: 157; Hutton, *Stations of the Sun*, 369.

52. IFC Ms. 949: 79.

53. IFC Ms. 949: 111.

54. IFC Ms. 949: 105.

55. Macleod Banks, *British Calendar Customs: Scotland*, 3: 162–63.

56. Ibid., 3: 114.

57. William Aiton, *A General View of the Agriculture of County of Ayr* (Glasgow: A. Napier, 1811), 154.

58. Leigh Eric Schmidt, *Consumer Rites. The Buying and Selling of American Holidays* (Princeton: Princeton University Press, 1995), 44.

59. *Gentleman's Magazine* 54 (1784): 343.

60. IFC Ms. 950: 184.

61. Robert Burns, *Halloween*, vi, lines 52–54. The "tap pickle" refers to the grain at the top of an oat stalk, although it also connotes Nelly's maidenhead. The divination in question is the drawing of oak stalks from the barn by young women. If the third stalk lacks a top-pickle, then the women in question will not be a virgin at marriage.

62. Wright, *British Calendar Customs* 3: 116–17; Macleod Banks, *British Calendar Customs: Scotland*: 3: 121–42.

63. Robert Fergusson, *Scots Poems*, ed. Alexander Law (Edinburgh: Oliver and Boyd, 1947), 48, from the Poem "Hallow-Fair."

64. IFC Ms. 949: 250.

65. Jack Santino, *The Hallowed Eve* (Lexington: University Press of Kentucky), 82.

66. *The Hallow Fair* (Stirling: W. Moore, 1826).

67. On this theme, see ibid., and *Hallow Fair, or the School for Lasses* (1784, n.p.) in Larpent Plays Collection, no. 653, Huntington Library, San Marino, California.

68. IFC Ms. 949: 143–44.

Chapter 3: Coming Over

1. Increase Mather, *A Testimony against Several Prophane and Superstitious Customs Now Practised by Some in New England* (London, 1687), 19, 41.

2. Cotton Mather, *The Wonders of the Invisible World: Being an Account of the Tryals of Several Witches Lately Executed in New England*, 3rd ed. (Boston, 1693).

3. Gregory S. Kealey, *Toronto Workers Respond to Industrial Capitalism 1867–1892* (Toronto: University of Toronto Press, 1980), ch. 7; Scot W. See, *Riots in New Brunswick: Orange Nativism and Social Violence in the 1840s* (Toronto: University of Toronto Press, 1993); Paul A. Gilje, *The Road to Mobocracy: Popular Disorder in New York City, 1763–1834* (Chapel Hill: Institute of Early American Culture and University of North Carolina Press, 1987), 125–38.

4. *Globe* (Toronto), 7 Nov. 1864; see also 5–12 Sept. 1860.

5. *Montreal Gazette*, 31 Oct. 1885.

6. *Montreal Gazette*, 1 Nov. 1900.

7. *Montreal Gazette*, 31 Oct. 1885.

8. *New York Herald*, 1 Nov. 1887; *Hamilton Spectator*, 1 Nov. 1892; *Montreal Gazette*, 1 Nov. 1903.

9. *Daily News* (Kingston), 1 Nov. 1876, 1881, 1890.

10. *Hamilton Spectator*, 26, 29 Oct. 1872; 30 Oct. 1873.

11. On this rivalry, see Kealey, *Toronto Workers*, ch. 7.

12. *Public Ledger* (Philadephia), 31 Oct., 2 Nov. 1865; 31 Oct. 1866.

13. *Montreal Gazette*, 1 Nov. 1886; *Daily News* (Kingston) 31 Oct. 1889.

14. *Chicago Daily Journal*, 31 Oct. 1907.

15. How urban the immigrant Irish were is a matter of historical controversy, but it appears that while the Irish did settle across North America, a disproportionate number lived in cities. In 1850, 33 percent of all Irish-Americans lived in the fifteen large cities; in 1890, 38 percent. The comparable figures for the whole population were 9 percent and 22 percent, respectively. David Doyle has calculated that in 1860, 44 percent of the 1.6 million Irish-Americans then lived in the leading forty-

three cities, compared with 12 percent of the total population. See David Noel Doyle, "The Irish Countryman Urbanized," *Journal of Urban History* 3 (1977): 391–408, and his review of Donald Akenson, *Being Had: Historians, Evidence and the Irish in North America* (Port Credit, Ontario: P. D. Meany, 1985) in *Irish Historical Studies* 30 (1987): 451–54.

16. *New York Herald*, 1 Nov. 1878.

17. *Daily News* (Kingston) 31 Oct. 1889.

18. *Daily British Whig* (Kingston), 30 Oct. 1897.

19. *New York Times*, 1 Nov. 1876.

20. *Montreal Gazette*, 1 Nov. 1872.

21. On the sexual allure of the city, see Christine Stansell, *City of Women: Sex and Class in New York, 1789–1860* (New York: Knopf, 1986). On leaving home, see Michael Katz, *The People of Hamilton, Canada West* (Cambridge, Mass.: Harvard University Press, 1975), ch. 5; Michael Katz and Ian Davey, "Youth and Early Industrialization in a Canadian City," in *Turning Points: Historical and Sociological Essays on the Family*, ed. John Demos and Sarane Spense Boocock (Chicago: University of Chicago Press, 1978), 81–120; Gordon Darroch, "Home and Away: Patterns of Residence, Schooling, and Work among Children and Never Married Young Adults, Canada, 1871 and 1901," *Journal of Family History* 26 (2001): 220–50.

22. See *Brockville Gazette*, 1 Dec. 1831. I thank Patrick Connor of York University for this reference.

23. *New York Herald*, 1 Nov. 1872. For an example of a mock-marriage at a Halloween party, see *Daily British Whig* (Kingston), 2 Nov. 1898.

24. *Daily News* (Kingston), 1 Nov. 1866.

25. *Daily British Whig* (Kingston), 1 Nov. 1884.

26. *Daily News* (Kingston), 1 Nov. 1893.

27. *Daily News* (Kingston), 31 Oct. 1889, 1 Nov. 1890.

28. *Weekly British Whig* (Kingston), 3 Nov. 1892.

29. *Evening Mail* (Halifax), 2 Nov. 1900.

30. *Evening Mail* (Halifax), 1 Nov. 1898.

31. For an account of these antics, see *Chicago Daily Tribune*, 1 Nov. 1901.

32. *Daily News* (Kingston), 1 Nov. 1872.

33. *Toronto Evening News*, 31 Oct. 1882.

34. *Daily News* (Kingston), 1 Nov. 1870.

35. *Daily News* (Kingston), 4 Nov. 1868.

36. *Hamilton Spectator*, 1 Nov. 1892.

37. *Daily British Whig*, 29 Oct., 2 Nov. 1903, 30 Oct. 1906; *Chatham Daily News*, 2 Nov. 1906.

38. *Daily British Whig*, 1 Nov. 1917.

39. *Chicago Daily Journal*, 31 Oct. 1905.

40. Arlington Heights *Daily Herald*, 11 Nov. 2001, p. 1, citing a local newspaper for 1902.

41. William S. Walsh, *Curiosities of Popular Customs*, 511.

42. Betty Smith, *A Tree Grows in Brooklyn* (New York: Harper & Row, 1943), 159. The action takes place around 1912. Thanks to Adele Perry of the University of Manitoba, Winnipeg, for this reference.

43. *Chicago Daily Tribune*, 1 Nov. 1901.

44. *Chicago Daily Journal*, 31 Oct. 1907.

45. *Chicago Daily Journal*, 1 Nov. 1907.

46. *New York Herald*, 1 Nov. 1904. For an instance of two young women being arrested for showering passers-by with flour, see *New York Herald*, 1 Nov. 1895. For arrests in Chicago, see *Chicago Daily Journal*, 1 Nov. 1907.

47. *Montreal Gazette*, 2 Nov. 1910.

48. *Chicago Daily Journal*, 1 Nov. 1907.

49. *Chicago Daily Tribune*, 2 Nov. 1900, 1901.

50. *Detroit News*, 1 Nov. 1904.

51. *Detroit News*, 1 Nov. 1905.

52. See account in *New York Herald*, 1 Nov. 1904.

53. Toronto *World*, 1 Nov. 1898, cited by Keith Walden, "Respectable Hooligans: Male Toronto College Students Celebrate Hallowe'en, 1884–1910," *Canadian Historical Review* 68 (1987): 11.

54. *Montreal Gazette*, 1 Nov. 1894.

55. *Daily Standard* (Kingston), 1 Nov. 1919, 1920.

56. *Daily Standard* (Kingston), 3 Nov. 1913.

57. Walden, "Respectable Hooligans," 23.

58. *Queen's University Journal* (1 Nov. 1904): 55.

59. *New York Herald*, 3 Nov. 1903.

60. Americans conventionally attribute the celebration of Halloween to the Irish immigrants, but its significance to Scottish immigrants was also admitted. See *New York Herald*, 31 Oct. 1872.

61. Kingston *Daily British Whig*, 30 Oct. 1875; *New York Herald*, 1 Nov. 1895.

62. Toronto *Mail and Empire*, 1 Nov. 1898.

63. New Orleans *Daily Picayune*, 1 Nov. 1898. I thank Dr. Helen Wilcox of the University of Groningen for the information about Martinmass.

64. *New York Herald*, 1 Nov. 1903, 1905; *Montreal Gazette*, 2 Nov. 1903.

65. *Chicago Daily Tribune*, 1 Nov. 1900; *Chicago Daily Journal*, 1 Nov. 1904.

66. *Montreal Gazette*, 2 Nov. 1908.

67. *Los Angeles Times*, 30, 31 Oct. 1910; *San Francisco Chronicle*, 1 Nov. 1910.

68. *Toronto Evening News*, 6 Nov. 1883; George William Douglas, *The American*

Book of Days (New York: H. W. Wilson, 1937), 555. On Pope's Day in colonial America, see Gilje, *Road to Mobocracy*, 25–30.

69. Tape 72–273/C 1471, Memorial University of Newfoundland, Folklore Archives (hereafter MUNFLA).

70. MUNFLA, FSC 74–103/002.

71. Joseph Reidy, "'Negro Election Day' and Black Community Life in New England, 1750–1860," *Marxist Perspectives* 1 (1978): 102–17.

72. Information provided by Gerry Hallowell, former senior editor of University of Toronto Press.

73. Stephen Nissenbaum, *The Battle for Christmas* (New York: A. Knopf, 1996), 101.

74. Ibid., 98. See also Gilje, *Road to Mobocracy*, 253–60.

75. On the embourgeoisment of Christmas and the braiding of commerce and religion, see Leigh Schmidt, *Consumer Rites*, ch. 3.

76. Susan Davis, "'Making Night Hideous': Christmas Revelry and Public Order in Nineteenth-Century Philadelphia," *American Quarterly* 34 (Summer 1982): 197.

77. Hennig Cohen and Tristram Potter Coffin, eds., *The Folklore of American Holidays* (Detroit: Gale Research, 1987), 224, citing the *New York Folklore Quarterly* 15 (1959): 112.

78. Roy Rosenzweig, *Eight Hours for What We Will: Workers and Leisure in an Industrial City, 1870–1920* (New York: Cambridge University Press, 1985), 74–81.

79. Thomas E. Hill, *Manual of Social and Business Forms* (Chicago: Standard Book, 1887), 253–54, cited in *Folklore of American Holidays*, 224.

80. Douglas, *American Book of Days*, 589.

81. Alice Dunbar-Nelson, *Give Us Each Day: The Diary of Alice Dunbar-Nelson*, ed. Gloria T. Hull (New York: W. H. Norton, 1984), 279.

82. On Mardi Gras in New Orleans and Mobile, see Samuel Kinser, *Carnival, American Style* (Chicago and London: University of Chicago Press, 1990); James Gill, *Lords of Misrule: Mardi Gras and the Politics of Race in New Orleans* (Jackson: University Press of Mississippi, 1997); and Joseph Roach, *Cities of the Dead: Circum-Atlantic Performance* (New York: Columbia University Press, 1996).

83. Kinser, *Carnival*, 92; Gilje, *Road to Mobocracy*, 257.

84. *North American Review* 84 (April 1857): 335, 353.

85. *Godey's Lady Book and Magazine* 68 (Oct. 1864): 358.

86. Lettie C. Van Derveer, *Halloween Happenings* (Boston: W. H. Baker, 1921); Schmidt, *Consumer Rites*, 260.

87. New Orleans *Daily Picayune*, 2 Nov. 1898.

88. Walter Pritchard Eaton, "Pungkins," *Outing* 61 (Oct. 1912): 33, cited in Tad Tuleja, "Trick or Treat: Pre-Texts and Contexts," in Jack Santino, ed., *Halloween and Other Festivals of Death and Life* (Knoxville: University of Tennessee Press, 1994), 87.

89. *Chicago Record*, 1 Nov. 1894; see also *Chicago Daily Journal*, 31 Oct. 1898.

90. Marie Irish, *Hallowe'en Hilarity* (Dayton, Ohio: Paine, 1924), 33.

91. Kingston, *Daily British Whig*, 1 Nov. 1911.

92. On cats, see Robert Darnton, *The Great Cat Massacre and Other Episodes in French Cultural History* (New York: Vintage, 1985), 92–96.

93. Van Derveer, *Halloween Happenings*, 14.

94. Kingston, *Daily British Whig*, 30 Oct. 1920.

95. *Kingston Standard*, 1 Nov. 1920.

Chapter 4: Razor in the Apple

1. *Toronto Daily Star*, 1 Nov. 1937.

2. *Winnipeg Free Press*, 1 Nov. 1930.

3. *Winnipeg Free Press*, 1 Nov. 1933.

4. *Vancouver Sun*, 1 Nov. 1932.

5. Toronto *Evening Telegram*, 2 Nov. 1936.

6. Overly domineering and swaggering.

7. *Vancouver Sun*, 2 Nov. 1934.

8. Toronto *Evening Telegram*, 1 Nov. 1933.

9. *Vancouver Sun*, 1 Nov. 1937.

10. *Los Angeles Times*, 1 Nov. 1959; I thank Betsy Broun, the director of the Smithsonian American Art Museum, for the information on "Neewollah" [Halloween spelt backwards.]

11. *Winnipeg Free Press*, 1 Nov. 1938.

12. Toronto *Evening Telegram*, 1 Nov. 1928.

13. Toronto *Evening Telegram*, 1 Nov. 1938.

14. *New York Daily News*, 2 Nov. 1931; *New York Herald*, 1 Nov. 1934. There had been a race riot on Halloween in Harlem in 1912, when young African-Americans had showered some white girls with flour, and their boyfriends retaliated. See *New York Herald*, 1 Nov. 1912.

15. *Vancouver Sun*, 1 Nov. 1935, 1939, 1940.

16. Toronto *Evening Telegram*, 1 Nov. 1934.

17. Toronto *Evening Telegram*, 1 Nov. 1939, 1940.

18. Toronto *Globe*, 1 Nov. 1945.

19. Toronto *Evening Telegram*, 1 Nov. 1945.

20. For accounts of the riot, see Toronto *Globe*, 1, 2 Nov. 1945; Toronto *Evening Telegram*, 1 Nov. 1945; *Winnipeg Free Press*, 1 Nov. 1945; *London Evening Free Press*, 1 Nov. 1945.

21. Toronto *Globe*, 2 Nov. 1945.

22. Toronto *Evening Telegram*, 1 Nov. 1945.

23. Toronto *Evening Telegram*, 31 Oct 1938. Here described as "many of heavier years."

24. *Vancouver Sun*, 1 Nov. 1933; Toronto *Evening Telegram*, 1 Nov. 1932.

25. Congressional Committee on the Judiciary, 20 July 1950, report no. 2131. I thank Jeet Heer of York University for obtaining a copy of this report for me.

26. Pledging was not new. It had been proposed in the Chicago school system as early as 1925. See Tad Tuleja, "Trick or Treat: Pre-Texts and Contexts," in Santino, ed., *Halloween*, 88.

27. *New York Times*, 25 July 1950, p. 50; 15 Oct 1950, part 6, p. 40.

28. Toronto *Globe*, 2 Nov. 1945.

29. *Vancouver Sun*, 1 Nov. 1938.

30. I owe this information to Professor Joseph Boyle, the principal of St. Michael's College, University of Toronto.

31. Enyl Jenkins, ed., *The Book of American Traditions* (New York: Crown, 1996), 255.

32. Gregory P. Stone, "Halloween and the Mass Child," *American Quarterly* 11 (1959): 374.

33. See J. N. Harris, "Quiet Hallowe'en," *Saturday Night*, 9 Nov. 1946, p. 24.

34. Stone, "Halloween and the Mass Child," 470.

35. Leigh Eric Schmidt, "The Commercialization of the Calendar: American Holidays and the Culture of Consumption, 1870–1930," *Journal of American History* 78 (Dec. 1991): 913–15. For an advertisement specifically linking Halloween house-visiting with consumerism, see *Toronto Daily Star*, 29 Oct. 1931.

36. Toronto *Evening Telegram*, 31 Oct., 1 Nov. 1940; *Winnipeg Free Press*, 1 Nov. 1944.

37. *New York Times*, 26 Aug. 1952, p. 28.

38. Information provided by Dr. Victoria Heftler of York University, Toronto.

39. *New York Times*, 29 Oct. 1954, p. 22.

40. *New York Times*, 27 Oct., 1 Nov. 1957, 24 Jan. 1958.

41. *New York Times*, 30 Oct. 1958, p. 61.

42. *New York Times*, 27 Oct. 1957, p. 58.

43. *Toronto Daily Star*, 30 Oct. 1958, p. 19.

44. *Gladstone Comic Album No. 23* (Prescott, Arizona, 1952).

45. *Los Angeles Times*, 2 Nov. 1959.

46. Information provided by David Thompson, of York University, Toronto.

47. *Los Angeles Times*, 4 Nov. 1959. The incident was widely reported in the *San Francisco Chronicle*.

48. Joel Best and Gerald T. Horiuchi, "The Razor Blade in the Apple: The Social Construction of Urban Legends," *Social Problems* 32 (1985): 488–99.

49. Cited by Best and Horiuchi, "Urban Legends," 488.

50. Catherine Harris Ainsworth, "Hallowe'en," *New York Folklore Quarterly* 29 (Sept. 1973): 179–80.

51. *New York Times*, 28 Oct., 2 Nov. 1982.

52. *Vancouver Sun*, 1 Nov. 1982.

53. *La Presse* (Montreal), 1 Nov. 1982; *Halifax Chronicle Herald*, 1 Nov. 1982; *Ottawa Citizen*, 1 Nov. 1982; *Vancouver Sun*, 1 Nov. 1982. For razor-in-the-apple stories prior to 1982, see, e.g., the *Hamilton Spectator*, 1 Nov. 1977, 1978.

54. Montreal *Gazette*, 1 Nov. 1982.

55. Bill Ellis, "'Safe' Spooks: New Halloween Traditions in Response to Sadism Legends," in Santino, ed., *Halloween*, 24–44; *Washington Post*, 31 Oct. 1984.

56. *Washington Post*, 31 Oct. 1985. The poll was conducted by the *Washington Post* and *ABC News* just prior to Halloween in 1985.

57. *New York Times*, 30 Oct. 1982.

58. Best and Horiuchi, "Urban Legends," 493n. Before 1967, half of the reported incidents in Best and Horiuchi's sample involved over-the-counter or prescription drugs.

59. Sylvia Grider, "The Razor Blades in the Apples Syndrome," in Paul Smith, ed. *Perspectives on Contemporary Legend* (Sheffield: University of Sheffield, 1984), 128–40; Jan Harold Brunard, *Curses! Broiled Again! The Hottest Urban Legends Going* (New York: Norton, 1989), 51–54; Best and Horiuchi, "Urban Legends," 488–99.

60. New Orleans *Times Picayune*, 31 Oct. 1975.

61. Best and Horiuchi, "Urban Legends," 491.

62. Cited in William H. Chafe and Harvard Sitkoff, eds., *A History of Our Time: Readings on Postwar America*, 2nd ed. (New York: Oxford University Press, 1987), 143.

63. Margaret A. Zahn and Patricia L McCall, "Trends and Patterns of Homicide in the 20th-Century United States," in M. Dwayne Smith and Margaret A. Zahn, eds., *Homicide: A Sourcebook of Social Research* (Thousand Oaks, Calif.: Sage, 1999), 9–27.

64. *New York Times*, 19 Oct. 1974, p. 26.

65. Daphne Spain, "Balancing Act," in *America's Demographic Tapestry*, ed. James W. Hughes and Joseph J. Seneca (New Brunswick, N.J.: Rutgers University Press, 1999), 165.

66. *Washington Post*, 31 Oct. 1984.

67. Ainsworth, "Hallowe'en," 184.

68. On this theme see Olivier Zunz, *The Changing Face of Inequality: Urbanization, Industrial Development and Immigrants in Detroit, 1880–1920* (Chicago: University of Chicago Press, 1982).

69. Paul Gilje, *Rioting in America* (Bloomington: Indiana University Press, 1996), 155–61.

70. Tamar Jacoby, *Someone Else's House: America's Unfinished Struggle for Integration* (New York: Basic Books, 1998), 238.

71. According to Jacoby, 40 percent of all commerce, retail and wholesale, moved beyond the city limits in the period 1950–75. Jacoby, *Someone Else's House*, 301.

72. Jacoby, *Someone Else's House*, 301–2.

73. *Detroit Free Press*, 30 Oct. 1990.

74. *Detroit Free Press*, 25 Oct. 1986.

75. *Detroit Free Press*, 30 Oct. 1986.

76. Ze'ev Chafets, *Devil's Night and Other True Tales of Detroit* (New York: Random House, 1990).

77. *Detroit Free Press*, 30 Oct. 1990.

78. *Winnipeg Free Press*, 30 Oct. 1950.

79. *Winnipeg Free Press*, 1 Nov. 1950.

Chapter 5: Halloween Goes to Hollywood

1. *Detroit Free Press*, 28 Oct. 1991.

2. *Detroit Free Press*, 30 Oct. 1987.

3. *Detroit Free Press*, 28 Oct. 1991.

4. *Washington Post*, 31 Oct. 1984. For the House of Ghostly Horrors, see *Pittsburgh Post-Gazette*, 28 Oct. 1988. For the spooky park, actually Prospect Park, Brooklyn, see *Village Voice*, 30 Oct. 1984, under "Cheap Thrillers."

5. *Wall Street Journal*, 29 Oct. 1991.

6. See www.haunted house.org under Ohio, where one haunted house reported 43,000 visitors in twenty-two nights in 1998.

7. Rhona J. Berenstein, "'It Will Thrill You, It May Shock You, It Might Even Horrify You': Gender, Reception, and Classic Horror Cinema," in Barry Keith Grant, ed., *The Dread of Difference: Gender and the Horror Film* (Austin: University of Texas Press, 1996), 124.

8. Bram Stoker, *Dracula* (Oxford: World Classics, 1983), 4–5. Stoker's original first chapter for the novel took place on Walpurgis Night, or May Day eve, when the dead purportedly walk the land as on Halloween. By the 1990s the chapter was included in an anthology of horror stories entitled *Murder for Halloween*, ed. Michele Slung and Roland Hartman (New York: Warner Books, 1994).

9. Toronto *Evening Telegram*, 1 Nov. 1938; Les Daniels, *Living in Fear: A History of Horror in the Mass Media* (New York: Scribner, 1975), 144.

10. Jack Santino, *New Old-Fashioned Ways* (Knoxville: University of Tennessee Press, 1996), 38; *Shock SuspenStories* 2 (Dec. 1950); Anthony Boucher, "Trick or Treat," in *Murder for Halloween*, 324. On comic censorship, see Les Daniels, *Living in Fear*, 158–63.

11. *Toronto Daily Star*, 30 Oct. 1958. The two adaptations were *Cat on a Hot Tin Roof*, starring Burl Ives, Elizabeth Taylor, and Paul Newman, and *The Old Man and the Sea*, starring Spencer Tracy.

12. *Toronto Star*, 31 Oct. 1968.

13. *Washington Post*, 3 Nov. 1986.

14. *Them!* (1954), a story of radioactive mutant giant ants, would be one exception to this rule; Alfred Hitchcock's *Psycho* (1960) was another.

15. Isabel Cristina Pinedo, *Recreational Terror: Women and the Pleasures of Horror Film Viewing* (Albany: State University of New York Press, 1997), 18.

16. Carol Clover, "Her Body, Himself: Gender in the Slasher Film," *Representations* 20 (Fall 1987): 192, 224; Pinedo, *Recreational Terror*, 72, 151n; Vera Dika, *Games of Terror: Halloween, Friday the 13th, and the Films of the Stalker Genre* (Rutherford, N.J.: Fairleigh Dickinson University Press, 1990), 142, disputes this.

17. For an illuminating discussion of horror as a post-Enlightenment phenomenon, see Noel Carroll, *The Philosophy of Horror, or, The Paradoxes of the Heart* (New York and London: Routledge, 1990), 12–35.

18. Robin Wood, *Hollywood from Vietnam to Reagan* (New York: Cambridge University Press, 1986), 78. See also Clive Barker, "On Horror and Subversion," in Clive Bloom, ed., *Gothic Horror* (New York: St. Martin's, 1998), 99–101.

19. Tony Williams, *Hearths of Darkness: The Family in the American Horror Film* (Madison, N.J.: Fairleigh Dickinson University Press, 1996), 219. Williams's suggestion that the film signals the "victory of patriarchal corporate control" ignores the contradictions in Cochran's macabre scheme.

20. For discussions of the camera work in *Halloween*, see J. P. Tellote, "Through a Pumpkin's Eye: The Reflexive Nature of Horror," in Gregory Waller, ed., *American Horrors: Essays on the Modern American Horror Film* (Urbana and Chicago: University of Illinois Press, 1987), 114–28; Carol J. Clover, *Men, Women, and Chain Saws: Gender in the Modern Horror Film* (Princeton, N.J.: Princeton University Press, 1992), ch. 4; Dika, *Games of Terror*.

21. Kim Newman, *Nightmare Movies* (London: Bloomsbury, 1984), 143–44.

22. Wood, *Hollywood*, 193–94; Williams, *Hearths of Darkness*, 216.

23. *Village Voice*, 6 Nov. 1978, pp. 67, 70. Carpenter's stabbing scenes are clearly derivative of *Psycho*, and, indeed, his heroine, Laurie Strode, is played by Jamie Lee Curtis, the daughter of *Psycho*'s first victim, Janet Leigh. The indebtedness to Romero's film comes largely in the shape of the implacable, zombie-like assailant, Michael Myers.

24. Newman, *Nightmare Movies*, 143. The film eventually grossed $55m. See www.halloweenmovies.com.

25. Mick Martin and Marsha Porter, *Video Movie Guide: 1987* (New York: Ballantine, 1988), 690, cited in Clover, *Men, Women, and Chain Saws*, 184.

26. Clover, *Men, Women, and Chain Saws*, 189.

27. Williams, *Hearths of Darkness*, ch. 9; Tony Williams, "Trying to Survive on the Darker Side: 1980s Family Horror," in *Dread of Difference*, 164–80. See also Wood, *Hollywood*, ch. 9, whose argument is similar.

28. Jonathan Lake Crane, *Terror and Everyday Life* (Thousand Oaks, Calif.: Sage, 1994), 5.

29. Ibid., 157.

30. *Boston Globe*, 1 Nov. 1988.

31. *New York Times*, 30 Oct. 1991.

32. Umberto Eco, *Travels in Hyperreality*, trans. William Weaver (London: Picador, 1987), 8.

33. New Orleans *Times Picayune*, 1 Nov. 1976.

34. Jean Baudrillard, *Simulations*, trans. Paul Foss, Paul Patton, and Philip Beitchman (New York: Semiotext(e), 1983), 24.

Chapter 6: Stepping Out

1. *Washington Post*, 31 Oct. 1983.

2. *Time Magazine*, vol. 122 (31 Oct. 1988): 82.

3. Ibid.

4. Russell W. Belk, "Carnival, Control, and Corporate Culture in Contemporary Halloween Celebrations," in Santino, ed., *Halloween*, 106.

5. Philadelphia *Public Ledger*, 2 Nov. 1865.

6. *Montreal Gazette*, 2 Nov. 1931.

7. Raymond McGrath of the American Beer Institute noted in 1995 that 80 percent of all costumes rented for Halloween were worn by adults. See *Toronto Globe and Mail*, 20 Oct. 1995, p. A20.

8. *Washington Post*, 23 Oct., 6 Nov. 1983.

9. *Halifax Chronicle Herald*, 29 Oct. 1990.

10. M. M. Bakhtin, *Rabelais and His World*, trans. Helen Iswolsky (Bloomington: Indiana University Press, 1984), 316–44, 362–67. See also the useful commentary in Simon Dentith, *Bakhtinian Thought* (London and New York: Routledge, 1995), ch. 3.

11. Kugelmass, *Masked Culture*, 180–81.

12. *Washington Post*, 31 Oct. 1983, 1 Nov. 1987; *National Review* 41 (24 Nov. 1989): 57.

13. On this theme, see Max Boas and Steve Chain, *Big Mac: The Unauthorized Story of McDonald's* (New York: Mentor, 1976).

14. *Washington Post*, 1 Nov. 1982, p. C1.

15. *Washington Post*, 1 Nov. 1985.

16. *Washington Post*, 1 Nov. 1988.

17. *Halifax Chronicle-Herald*, 2 Nov. 1987.

18. www.buycostumes.com, mid-Oct. 2001.

19. *Pittsburgh Post-Gazette*, 1 Nov. 1975.

20. Jack Kugelmass, "Designing the Greenwich Village Parade," in Santino, ed., *Halloween*, 191, 207.

21. Kugelmass, *Masked Culture*, 96–97.

22. Cited in David Caute, *The Year of the Barricades* (New York: Harper and Row, 1988), 267. See also John D'Emilio and Estelle B. Freedman, *Intimate Matters: A History of Sexuality in America* (New York: Harper and Row, 1988), 308–18.

23. *Michigan Daily*, 31 Oct. 1970.

24. *Village Voice*, 4 Nov. 1971, p. 51.

25. I owe this information to Dr. Cynthia Wright of Toronto.

26. See Victor Turner, *From Ritual to Theatre* (New York: Performing Arts Journal, 1982), 28, 53–56, where Halloween is described as a "liminoid" festival.

27. *Montreal Gazette*, 2 Nov. 1931.

28. *Mail and Empire* (Toronto), 1 Nov. 1898.

29. Marc Stein, *City of Sisterly and Brotherly Loves: Lesbian and Gay Philadelphia, 1945–1972* (Chicago and London: University of Chicago Press, 2000), 105.

30. Ibid., 107.

31. Ibid., 111.

32. *San Francisco Examiner*, 1 Nov. 1971, cited by Mary O'Drain, "San Francisco's Gay Halloween," *International Folklore Review* 4 (1986): 90.

33. *Village Voice*, 4 Nov. 1971.

34. Jack Kugelmass, "Imagining Culture: New York City's Village Halloween Parade," in *Feasts and Celebrations in North American Ethnic Communities*, ed. Ramon A. Gutierrez and Geneviève Fabre (Albuquerque: University of New Mexico Press, 1995), 141–58.

35. Kugelmass, "Greenwich Village Parade," 191.

36. See Mary O'Drain, "San Francisco's Gay Halloween," *International Folklore Review* 4 (1986): 90–94.

37. *Body Politic* (Toronto) 1 (Nov./Dec. 1971): 10; 6 (Autumn 1972): 21.

38. *Body Politic* 3 (Nov. 1977): 8; *Toronto Star*, 1 Nov. 1973.

39. *Washington Post*, 1 Nov. 1990.

40. On Halifax, see Russell W. Belk, "Carnival, Control and Corporate Culture in Contemporary Halloween Celebrations," 111–15.

41. *Detroit Free Press*, 31 Oct. 1990.

42. See the introduction to Victor Turner, ed., *Celebration: Studies in Festivity and Ritual* (Washington: Smithsonian, 1982).

43. On the different kinds of liminality and their subversive potential, see Victor

Turner, "Variations on a Theme of Liminality," in *Blazing the Trail*, ed. Edith Turner (Tucson: University of Arizona Press, 1992), 48–65.

44. D. Keith Mayo, "The New York Halloween Parade," *National Review* 41 (24 Nov. 1989): 57. See also Kugelmass, "Imagining Culture," 141–58, and *Masked Culture*.

45. Sean Wilentz, *Chants Democratic: New York City and the Rise of the American Working Class 1788–1850* (New York: Oxford University Press, 1984); Len Travers, *Celebrating the Fourth: Independence Day and the Rites of Nationalism in the Early Republic* (Amherst: University of Massachusetts Press, 1997).

46. Richard Behar, "Warlocks, Witches, and Swastikas," *Time Magazine* (29 Oct. 1988): 27–28, cited in Syliva Ann Grider, "Conservatism and Dynamism in the Contemporary Celebration of Halloween: Institutionalization, Commercialization, Gentrification," *Southern Folklore* 53 (1996): 4.

47. *New York Times*, 21 Nov. 1990.

48. *New York Times*, 2, 3, 5 Nov. 1990.

49. Emmanuel Le Roy Ladurie, *Carnival in Romans*, trans. Mary Feeney (New York: George Braziller, 1979), 316.

50. Robert Stam, *Subversive Pleasures: Bakhtin, Cultural Criticism and Film* (Baltimore: Johns Hopkins University Press, 1989), 95.

Chapter 7: Border Crossings

1. Information from my colleague Yves Frenette, of Glendon College, York University.

2. Steve H. Murdock, *An America Challenged: Population Change and the Future of the United States* (Boston: Westview Press, 1995), table 2.6.

3. See the video documentary *El Dia de los Muertos* (Institute of Texan Cultures, San Antonio, 1991).

4. Kay Turner and Pat Jasper, "Day of the Dead: The Tex-Mex Tradition," in Santino, ed., *Halloween*, 145–47. "Dead bread" has only recently been reintroduced in the Texan celebrations of the Day of the Dead.

5. F. Gonzalez-Crussi, *The Day of the Dead and Other Mortal Reflections* (New York: Harcourt Brace, 1993), 36.

6. *Ottawa Citizen*, 2 Nov. 1996, p. A7; Elizabeth Carmichael and Chloë Sayer, *The Skeleton at the Feast: The Day of the Dead in Mexico* (Austin: University of Texas Press, 1995), 119, 129–30.

7. *Time International* (2 Nov. 1988): 17.

8. Hallmark gift bags are made at the U.S.-owned Duro *maquiladora* in Rio Bravo. According to Lynda Yanz, the president of the trinational Coalition for Justice in the Maquiladoras, the police recently dispersed peaceful strikers at the factory,

190 Notes to Pages 143–150

threatening them with pistols and rifles. See Toronto *Globe and Mail*, 23 Aug. 2000, p. A15.

9. Nutini, *Todos Santos*, ch. 2.

10. See, e.g., Antonio de Herrera y Tardesillas, *The General History of the Vast Continent and Islands of America, Commonly Call'd, the West Indies*, 6 vols., 2nd ed. (London, 1740), 2: 377–78.

11. Stanley Brandes, "Sugar, Colonialism, and Death: On the Origins of Mexico's Day of the Dead," *Comparative Studies in Society and History* 39 (1997): 277–81, and his "Iconography in Mexico's Day of the Dead," *Ethnohistory* 45 (1998): 189–94; Juanita Garciagodoy, *Digging the Days of the Dead* (Niwot: University Press of Colorado, 1998), 119–27.

12. Herrera, *History of America*, 2: 380.

13. Cited by Nutini, *Todos Santos*, 87.

14. Cited in Chloë Sayer, *The Mexican Day of the Dead* (Boston: Shambhala, 1990), 80.

15. Brandes, "Sugar, Colonialism," 281–87.

16. *The Poetical Works of Robert Burns*, ed. Rev. Robert Aris Willmott (London and New York: Routledge, 1856), 62. I thank Sabina Flanagan and Wilf Prest of the University of Adelaide for this reference.

17. Wayland Hand, Anna Casetta, and Sondra B. Theaderman, *Popular Beliefs and Superstitions: A Compendium of American Folklore*, 3 vols. (Boston: G. K. Hall, 1981), passim.

18. Harry Middleton Hyatt, *Hoodoo—Conjuration—Witchcraft—Rootwork*, 4 vols. (Washington: Western, 1970) 1: 45–46.

19. Bettina Bradbury, *Working Families: Age, Gender, and Daily Survival in Industrializing Montreal* (Toronto: University of Toronto Press, 1993), 60, 73.

20. Colin M. MacLachlan and Jaime E. O. Rodriguez, *The Forging of the Cosmic Race: A Reinterpretation of Colonial Mexico* (Berkeley and Los Angeles: University of California Press, 1990), 287.

21. Nutini, *Todos Santos*, 367; Pierre Goubert, *Louis XIV and Twenty Million Frenchmen*, trans. Anne Carter (New York: Pantheon, 1970), 21.

22. From Eisenstein's *Memoirs*, cited by Sayer, *Mexican Day of the Dead*, 45.

23. John Greenleigh and Rosalind Rosoff Beimler, *The Days of the Dead* (San Francisco: Collins, 1991), 21.

24. Gonzalez-Crussi, *Day of the Dead*, 60–61.

25. S. M. Eisenstein, "Towards a Theory of Montage," in Michael Gleary and Richard Taylor, eds., *Selected Works*, 4 vols. (London: British Film Institute, 1988–94), 2: 45.

26. As was said of the 1867 celebrations of the Day of the Dead. See William H. Beezley, *Judas at the Jockey Club* (Lincoln: University of Nebraska Press), 102.

27. Cited in *J. G. Posada Messenger of Mortality*, ed. Julian Rothenstein (London: Redstone Press, 1989), 187.

28. Ibid., 14–15, 181.

29. Ibid., 187. See also Brandes, "Iconography in Mexico's Day of the Dead," 194–201.

30. Octavio Paz, *The Labyrinth of Solitude*, trans. Lysander Kemp, Yara Milos, and Rachel Phillips Belash (New York: Grove Press, 1985), 57–59.

31. Brandes, "Iconography in Mexico's Day of the Dead," 188.

32. Garciagodoy, *Digging the Days of the Dead*, 270–71. See also Nutini, *Todos Santos*, passim.

33. Carlos Fuentes, *A New Time for Mexico* (Berkeley and Los Angeles: University of California Press, 1997), 16–18.

34. Carmichael and Sayer, *The Skeleton at the Feast*, pp. 8–9, 142.

35. Beezley, *Judas at the Jockey Club*, 98; see also Edward Larocque Tinker, *Corridos and Calaveras* (Austin: University of Texas Press, 1961), 21, 25–26.

36. Carmichael and Sayer, *The Skeleton at the Feast*, plate 23a.

37. Ibid., plate 31; *Arizona Republic*, 3 Nov. 1999.

38. Information supplied by Professor Denis Paz of the University of North Texas, Denton.

39. *New York Times*, 16 Oct. 2001.

40. Garciagodoy, *Digging the Days of the Dead*, 155.

41. On these issues, see ibid., esp. chs. 3 and 10.

42. Stanley Brandes, *Power and Persuasion: Fiestas and Social Control in Rural Mexico* (Philadelphia: University of Pennsylvania Press, 1988), passim; www.mexoline.com/oaxaca/cantrera4.html.

43. Garciagodoy, *Digging the Days of the Dead*, 223–25. Superbarrio is a social activist in Mexico City who wears a costume inspired by professional wrestlers when he leads protests on behalf of the poor, the homeless, the marginal.

44. Ibid., 251–57.

Chapter 8: Halloween at the Millennium

1. *Martha Stewart Living: Holiday Halloween* (Oct. 2000), p. 50.

2. A. W. Sadler, "The Seasonal Context of Halloween: Vermont's Unwritten Law," in Santino, ed., *Halloween*, 170–86. The conjunction of Halloween with the opening of the hunting season in New Hampshire is also stressed in the recent movie *Affliction* (1998).

3. *U.S. News and World Report* 123/17 (3 Nov. 1997): 14.

4. Slung and Hartman, eds., *Murder for Halloween*, xiv.

5. Jenkins, ed., *American Traditions*, 264–67.

6. *Advertising Age* 69/37 (14 Sept. 1998): 4.

7. *Chronicle of Higher Education* (3 Nov. 2000): B4.

8. *Christian Science Monitor*, (31 Oct. 1996): 14.

9. *Atlanta Constitution*, 1 Nov. 2001, p. A18.

10. *Christian Science Monitor*, (31 Oct 1995), 13.

11. *Washington Post*, 30 Oct. 1998, p. B3.

12. *Orlando Sentinel*, 20 Oct. 2001, p. 8.

13. *Washington Post*, 30 Oct. 1998, p. B3.

14. See the film *Hell House* (Cantina Pictures/Mixed Greens, 2001), directed by George Ratcliff.

15. *New York Times*, 27 Oct. 1996, pp. E1, 3. Thanks to Bryan Palmer for this reference.

16. Kugelmass, *Masked Culture*, 21.

17. *New York Times*, 23 Oct. 1996, p. A1; *Florida Times*, 15 Oct. 2001, p. B1.

18. *Washington Post*, 1 Nov. 1982.

19. On the attack upon the beer industry, see *Christian Science Monitor* (26 Oct. 1995): 4.

20. Birmingham *Evening Mail*, 3 Nov. 2001, pp. 3, 13; *South Wales Echo*, 1, 2 Nov. 2001.

21. Schmidt, *Consumer Rites*, 298.

22. *St. Louis Post-Dispatch*, 17 Oct. 2001, p. C14.

23. *New York Times*, 16 Oct. 2001; *Portland Press Herald*, 1 Nov. 2001, p. 13A.

24. *Fort Worth Star-Telegram*, 2 Nov. 2001.

25. *Bangor Daily News*, 19 Oct. 2001; *Washington Post*, 22 Oct. 2001; *Cincinnati Post*, 20 Oct. 2001.

26. *Rocky Mountain News*, 16 Oct. 2001, p. 5A.

27. *St. Louis Post-Dispatch*, 14 Oct. 2001, p. B3.

28. See the remarks of Jim Berger Clay in the Syracuse *Post Standard*, 19 Oct. 2001, A13.

29. *St. Louis Post*, 21 Oct. 2001.

30. *Portland Press Herald*, 22 Oct. 2001; on governors discouraging treat-or-treating, see New Delhi, India, *Statesman*, 21 Oct. 2001.

31. *San Francisco Chronicle*, 21 Oct. 2001.

32. *Newsday*, 21 Oct. 2001, p. A53; *San Francisco Chronicle*, 21 Oct. 2001.

33. New Delhi, India, *Statesman*, 21 Oct. 2001.

34. *Baton Rouge Advocate*, 1 Nov. 2001, p. 4B.

35. *Hartford Courant*, 1 Nov. 2001, p. 18.

36. *New York Times*, 14 Oct. 2001, p. 1.

37. New Delhi *Statesman*, 21 Oct. 2001.

38. *San Francisco Chronicle*, 21 Oct. 2001.

39. *Wall Street Journal*, 19 Oct. 2001.

40. *Boston Herald*, 21 Oct. 2001.

41. *Richmond Times-Dispatch*, 15 Oct. 2001, p. B5.

42. *Washington Post*, 1 Nov. 2001, p. B1.

43. *Grand Rapids Press*, 1 Nov. 2001; *Sarasota Herald Tribune*, 20 Oct. 2001.

44. *San Diego Union-Tribune*, 20 Oct. 2001, p. B2.

45. *Los Angeles Times*, 1 Nov. 2001, p. B3.

46. For sales in Mexico City, see *Houston Chronicle*, 19 Oct. 2001.

47. *Pittsburgh Post-Gazette*, 5 Nov. 2001, p. D2; *Austin American Statesman*, 1 Nov. 2001, p. B1; *Wall Street Journal*, 19 Oct. 2001.

48. *Plain Dealer*, 21 Oct. 2001.

49. For some general reflections on the changing nature of commemorative practices, see Pierra Nora, "The Era of Commemoration," in Pierre Nora, ed., *Realms of Memory: III, Symbols*, trans. Arthur Goldhammer (New York: Columbia University Press, 1998), 609–37.

50. Michel Foucault, "Of Other Spaces," *Diacritics* 16 (Spring 1986): 22–27.

Index

Index   197